SMOKE IN THE COCKPIT

Smoke in the Cockpit

The Flying Adventures
of Don "Smokey" Patry

By H.J. Smith

NEWEST
PRESS

Library and Archives Canada Cataloguing in Publication
Smith, H. J. (Hugh John), 1959-

Smoke in the cockpit : the flying adventures of Don "Smokey" Patry / H.J. Smith.

Includes bibliographical references.

ISBN-13: 978-1-897126-07-3
ISBN-10: 1-897126-07-7

I. Patry, Don. 2. Bush pilots--Canada--Biography. 3. Bomber pilots--Canada--Biography. I. Title.

TL540.P38S65 2006   629.13092   C2006-903777-9

Editor for the press: Don Kerr
Cover and interior design: Ruth Linka
Cover image: D.V. Patry Collection
Author Photo: Caileigh Smith

Every effort has been made to obtain permissions for photographs. If there is an omission or error, the author and publisher would be grateful to be so informed.

  Canada Council Conseil des Arts
for the Arts du Canada   Canadian Patrimoine
Heritage canadien   edmonton arts council

NeWest Press acknowledges the support of the Canada Council for the Arts and the Alberta Foundation for the Arts, and the Edmonton Arts Council for our publishing program. We also acknowledge the financial support of the Government of Canada through the Book Publishing Industry Development Program (BPIDP) for our publishing activities.

NeWest Press
201–8540–109 Street
Edmonton, Alberta T6G 1E6
(780) 432-9427
www.newestpress.com

1 2 3 4 5 09 08 07 06

NeWest Press is committed to protecting the environment and to the responsible use of natural resources. This book is printed on 100% post-consumer recycled and ancient-forest-friendly paper. For more information, please visit www.oldgrowthfree.com.

PRINTED AND BOUND IN CANADA

Dedicated to Jack Sullivan. A promise made. A promise kept.

TABLE OF CONTENTS

Don 'Smokey' Patry, spring 1941, age 26, stands on the dock at
Charlie Lake, Fort St. John, BC, beside float plane CF-BMW.
D.V. Patry collection

PREFACE

My flying partner, John Joseph "Jack" Sullivan, earned his wings at the age of seventy-two. He had a lifelong love of aviation that was put on hold as he managed the responsibilities of being a farmer, husband, and father of six. However, with the help of his patient instructor, Hugh McDevitt, Jack achieved his dream sixty-seven years after he first saw a plane fly over Guelph, Ontario.

Jack was knowledgeable about airplanes and loved to talk flying, so when he met Don "Smokey" Patry, they quickly became friends. It didn't take Jack very long to realize that Smokey had been a participant in some very significant Canadian aviation history, and he was determined that these experiences be recorded. Time and again he would lament that "somebody should write down Don's stories before it's too late!"

Jack approached a well-known aviation writer, who told him he wasn't interested in an old pilot's stories, there were too many of them already. This made Jack mad and, I guess, a little desperate, because he asked if I'd do it. I knew nothing about writing, but Jack was so enthusiastic that I agreed. Anyway, I naively reasoned, how difficult can it be to record a couple of stories?

We began this project in April 2002. Don's experiences were not just old hangar tales—far from it. In his quiet, understated way, Don told his stories and the old days came alive again. If he drew a blank now and then, his wife, Irene, was more than able to fill in the details, since she had been there for every step of the journey.

Before I knew it, a couple of stories had grown into thirty, and this book started to take flight. I consider myself fortunate to have been along for the ride with a pilot and gentleman whose fascinating story deserves to be shared.

Enjoy *Smoke in the Cockpit*, the story we landed before it was too late.

—H.J. Smith

INTRODUCTION

"Somebody oughta make a movie about this guy!" This was the reaction from one reader of an early draft of *Smoke in the Cockpit*. I don't think Don "Smokey" Patry was a thrill-seeker, or that he consciously put himself in life-threatening situations. Nor would he have had any way of foreseeing the historical significance of the events he participated in. It was simply his destiny.

How else to explain his surviving, among other things, the forced landing, in fog, of his first commercial flight; his five-day winter walk out of the wilderness after busting up his plane on his first bush flying trip; his being stranded deep in the bush for three days until he rebuilt his engine with a rusty file; his successful forced landing of a loaded cargo plane on a lake with three inches of ice, when the weight of the plane should have required five; a night landing on a tiny lake with five passengers and ten more minutes of fuel; or his service with the Allied Ferry Command during the Second World War, which included zigzagging a bomber across the Atlantic Ocean in heavy cloud, guided by a hungover navigator and followed by three other bombers that he didn't even know were there!

In 1938 Smokey was the second pilot hired by the fledgling community-based Peace River Airways (PRA). After fifteen minutes of instruction on floatplane operation, he flew three and a half hours from Edmonton to Peace River and made a successful landing, his third ever on floats. While with Yukon Southern Air Transport (YSAT), he piloted the American surveyors who determined the route of the Alaska Highway. Before long he became chief pilot for upstart Canadian Pacific Airlines (CPA), led by Canadian aviation icon Grant McConachie. As a result of the Japanese attack on Pearl Harbour, he was assigned an emergency mission of transporting Royal Canadian Air Force ground crews to Alaska. For rescuing an injured B-26 pilot, he received a personal letter of thanks from a US Army Brigadier General. His discovery of the mountainside wreckage of a CPA passenger plane ended one of the largest aerial searches in Canadian history. For twenty-six years he was a captain with Canada's national airline, enduring engine failure, bomb threats, and bureaucracy.

Don was born in 1915 on a farm at Waugh, Alberta, the youngest of five children, with two brothers, Louis and Phillip, and two sisters, Laura and Catherine. He came by his sense of adventure naturally, as his parents, Joseph and Eliza, and his extended family had come by wagon train in 1902 from South Dakota, driving a herd of horses destined for the Peace River area of what is now known as Alberta. They got as far as Fort Edmonton, North West Territories, when Eliza's mother became ill and could travel no further. With few options left, they stopped about thirty miles north of Fort Edmonton, determined to make the best of the situation. Then disaster struck: disease ran through the herd and most of the horses died. Since there was now no reason to venture

Parents Joseph Vital Patry and Eliza Patry in front
of their frame home at Waugh, Alberta.
D.V. Patry collection

to Peace River, the decision was made to stay put and farm. The Patrys' home became a stopping place for travellers on the second night out from Fort Edmonton northbound on the Old Athabasca Trail.

Later, in 1905, Don's maternal grandparents, William and Catherine Waugh, opened a post office, and the settlement became known as Waugh, Alberta. The trek north wasn't his family's first adventure: his father was born in Beaumount, Quebec, and the family history there goes back to 1667, and before that to France. Don's mother was from South Dakota, and she had met and married Joseph there. When Don was twelve, the family moved from the farm into Edmonton. Although he didn't realize it at the time, this move would have a dramatic impact on his life: Edmonton had an airport buzzing with bush planes.

Don's brother-in-law Russ Thoman was the telegraph operator and lineman for Dominion Telegraph in Edmonton. At that time, the telegraph was the main means of communication for bush pilots, and Edmonton was the centre of activity for many flights, so Russ was well informed about their comings and goings. A safe return from a lengthy trip was often sufficient reason to throw a party, and as Russ

Don and siblings, Catherine, Laura, Phillip, and Louis.
D.V. Patry collection

was a sociable type, he liked to join in. No doubt a few tales of flying adventures were passed on to an impressionable young Don.

After the telegraph messages were received, they were delivered via bicycle by the telegraph boy, Chris Moon, who was a budding pilot himself, building up hours toward his commercial endorsement. To offset his flying costs, he would take passengers for a ride. For two dollars, Don got his first ride in an airplane on a cold, sunny day in late December 1935. The plane was a Gypsy Moth, and time has not diminished the memory for Don, especially the characteristic aroma

Don's first instructor,
Maurice Burbidge.
D.V. Patry collection

of aviation fuel and crankcase oil: "I can still smell that airplane." Upon landing, Don walked inside and immediately joined the Edmonton and Northern Alberta Aero Club. Established in 1927, it's one of the oldest flying clubs in North America.

Flying lessons in those days cost twelve dollars per hour dual, or eight dollars per hour solo. Fortunately for Don, his mother was supportive of his endeavours and helped him out with the costs. In 1936 he soloed after nine and a half hours, and soon he had built up his time to the twenty-five hours required to get his licence. His first passenger was his girlfriend, later to be his wife, Irene Carson. His second passenger was his sister Laura MacDonald.

In 1937, Don started his professional flying career as a twenty-two-year-old bush pilot in northern Alberta, British Columbia, and the North West Territories, an area the rudimentary charts of the day described as "uncharted mountainous territory." He navigated by the

Don and mother Eliza. Mrs. Patry
financed the flying lessons.
D. V. Patry collection

rivers and the sun, with little help from the few and, at best, unreliable instruments available to him. Decades later, he retired from Air Canada with twenty-five thousand hours as pilot in command. In between were enough adventures for several lifetimes. While Don would modestly sum up his accomplishments as, "I never left a plane in the bush," there's much more to be told. The following stories provide a unique glimpse into Canadian aviation history, and a firsthand account of the fascinating career of Smokey Patry.

CHAPTER ONE: **THE EARLY YEARS**

First Planes

Early in his flying career, Don tagged himself with a nickname, more or less accidentally. "About twenty-six of us soloed at the old Edmonton Flying Club, and they were having a party for us. Everybody was calling each other by their last name, so I was Patry. So I said to this one fella, 'I don't like being called Patry, especially by my friends. We've all gone through this ground school and flying course together, so call me Smokey Joe or anything but Patry!' Well, it stuck, and then got shortened to Smokey, and then just Smoke. A lot of people figured it was because I smoked cigars, but that's how it actually happened, and it stuck for all these years."

Shortly after he started flying, Don's next door neighbour, Mr. Jim Cooney, said he needed to talk to him. Jim was concerned about the safety of this flying business and the welfare of the boy he had watched grow up. So he offered help in the only way he knew how. He gave Don his Saint Christopher medal. Saint Christopher is the patron saint of travellers, and Jim hoped it would keep the young lad safe. From that day on, the medal was with Don on every flight, and on more than one occasion Saint Christopher's help was very much needed and appreciated.

Don proudly wears his new wings.
D.V. Patry collection

Don acquired his first plane more or less by accident. A club member had a mishap with a Cirrus Moth, G-CAUE and the club sold the damaged plane to Don and Frank Burton for one hundred and twenty-five dollars. Frank was a licenced pilot and the engineer for the flying club. He had a "B and D" engineering rating that authorized him to sign off for airframe and engine repairs. So Frank led the project, and with Don's help, rebuilt the Moth. AUE had a 75-horsepower inline four-cylinder Cirrus engine, plywood fuselage, and large, thin tires with a straight axle that "made it nasty to land in a wheat field." Once it was airworthy again, Don flew it to help build time. He also flew weather flights for the Ministry of Transport (MOT) in the flying club's Fleet Finch, taking off at dawn and climbing as high as the Finch would go (over 10,000 feet). The plane was equipped with devices to record weather conditions, and the "met man" would later analyze this information to produce his weather reports. Despite the lack of oxygen, these flights were usually routine. At least one of them, however, was anything but.

Don had descended in poor visibility, trusting that things would improve by the time he reached the ground. After dropping down about as low as he thought prudent, he was still in snow flurries and not too

DeHavilland Cirrus Moth G-CAUE , Edmonton Airfield. Don's first airplane.
Previously owned by the Edmonton and Northern Alberta Aero Club.
D.V. Patry collection

certain where he was, but upon spotting a stubble field, he decided to land. He got a bit of a surprise when he suddenly saw a haystack go past the wing! After landing safely, he heard a train whistle, took off again in the direction of the noise, and managed to locate the train tracks, which he followed for a short time until he saw a grain elevator. As soon as he read the name of the town on the side of the elevator, he knew where he was and it was a simple matter to follow the tracks back toward the airport. While Don didn't prepare the weather reports, if he did, that day's would have been snow flurries, heavy at times, with intermittent haystacks and chance of locomotives.

Between flying the Moth and the Fleet Finch, Don accumulated the fifty hours required for his commercial licence, which he obtained in 1937. With this endorsement, he could now legally fly charter flights for hire, which got him into his next white-knuckle flight. A doctor whose wife was ill hired Don to fly him to Calgary, where she was being treated. The flight down was unremarkable, and the following day Don left for Edmonton at daybreak in visual flight rules (VFR) conditions. Encountering fog, he elected once again to follow the railroad tracks

Disassembled Cirrus Moth after a forced landing between Calgary and Edmonton, 1937. Don is standing at the far right.
D.V. Patry collection

as a precautionary move. This worked nicely at first, but the fog got thicker and the reduced visibility necessitated a reduction in altitude in order to maintain visual contact with the ground. And so the drill went: the fog got thicker, Don went lower, and soon he was feeling very uncomfortable, with little forward visibility and even less below. Then it got a whole lot worse as he realized that he had just flown *past* a grain elevator, not *over* it. "That kind of scared me."

Then and there, Don decided to land in the soup, and hope for the best. He descended slowly, not knowing what was in front of him, and touched down, cut the throttle, and pulled the stick back. Just when it looked like he had managed to pull a rabbit out of the hat, he felt AUE buck, drop suddenly, and belly flop to a stop. Later he discovered he had bounced through a creek and the impact had torn off the undercarriage. As people from nearby ran over to see what all the noise was about, Don could only see their legs, as the rest of them was hidden in the fog! AUE completed the trip to Edmonton on the back of a truck, and was eventually restored to flying condition.

The Trapper's Deal

The winter of 1937–38 saw Don hired as pilot for two trappers and traders known as "the Jacks," Jack Mulholland and Jack Sime. Adventurers and risk-takers of the highest order, these characters got by on credit lines, goodwill, optimism, guts, and rum. Mulholland had a trading post at Nahanni, and Sime had one at Fort Nelson. Sime, a native of Edinburgh, Scotland, was known as the trapper's friend and it was said that he never turned a fellow trapper down for credit. The first order of business was to acquire an airplane. Don made a trip to Sudbury, Ontario, to inspect one that was for sale, but it was not suitable. Eventually he and the Jacks found a Fairchild KR-34 biplane, CF-AUU, that had been used by a mining company before it went broke, and they purchased it on credit. It came equipped with wheels, skis, and floats, giving it the versatility necessary for a bush plane. Tempering this attribute was its narrow gear and tendency to turn sideways or ground loop if the pilot let the airplane's movements get ahead of his reactions for even a second during landing. Unfortunately, this was to happen sooner rather than later.

Frank Burton flew the KR-34 to Cooking Lake, which was the float base for Edmonton (and the location of a great dance pavilion that Don and the other pilots frequented). Here, Frank intended to install the floats. During the landing roll, the plane turned sideways, the wing touched the ground, and a bottom spar broke. Frank and Don repaired the damage and once again Frank flew to Cooking Lake—and once again ground looped and broke a spar. The good news was that by now they were experienced in the required repairs, experience that Don would put to good use sooner than anyone imagined.

Frank survived his mishaps unharmed, but he'd had enough of the KR-34, and decided to hand the reins to Don for the third attempt to land at the Cooking Lake strip. This landing was managed without incident, and in short order they had the floats installed. Having never flown on floats before, Don was naturally a little apprehensive. He was advised to "go talk to Bud." So he consulted Bud Potter, the secretary of the flying club, who had acquired some float time while flying for Consolidated Mining. "I did what Bud told me to do, which wasn't much. 'Hang on to the float strut to hand prop' and 'watch out for porpoising.' That was my float training." While the training was minimal, it must have been enough, as the first takeoff and landing were successful. After accumulating a grand total of two hours on floats,

Frank Burton and Don Patry,
in front of the Peace River Airlines
office, Peace River, Alberta, 1938.
D.V. Patry collection

the farm boy turned bush pilot was ready to challenge the north. If he knew what the future held, he might have had second thoughts.

Department of Transport regulations made it mandatory to have an aircraft engineer inspect and sign off the plane as airworthy each day. A fellow by the name of Red McLaughlin had taken on the job as engineer for the venture, and he came equipped with a Model T Ford tool box filled to capacity with the various wrenches, pliers, and knuckle dusters required to fulfill his duties. While the presence of a mechanic was reassuring to Don, the thought of the weight of all those tools added to an already considerable load was not. Skis were tied to the lower wings and would be installed on the plane once the ground was snow-covered. The baggage compartment was full, and a ten-gallon can of gas was sandwiched in the middle of the front seat between the two passengers. Just as they were about ready to head out, word came from McKenzie Air Service that the rivers were starting to run ice, so the trip was scrubbed, the floats replaced with wheels, and the plane flown back to Edmonton. Shortly thereafter, Red got cold feet about the adventure and backed out, and a replacement had to be found.

Jack Mulholland heard that an engineer in Calgary by the name of Johnny Laskowski was available for hire, so he and Don flew the Fairchild down to see him. Because of a headwind, the trip took longer than expected and it was dark by the time they were southeast of Calgary, looking for the field but without much success. Suddenly they saw a light go on and sighted the field. Don set up his approach and landed, just missing an unseen culvert. In short order, the fellow who had turned on the light after hearing them fly over appeared, and he gave them a dressing-down for landing at night. Jack phoned Laskowski, who agreed to be the new engineer and to fly back with them the next day.

The throttle and mixture control on the KR-34 are located low on the left-hand side of the cockpit. During takeoff on the trip back to Edmonton, Don's left sleeve caught the mixture control, and suddenly the engine quit. They were fifty feet in the air and the only noise to be heard was the pounding of their hearts. Don immediately realized the problem and reset the mixture. The noise returned and they flew on, but unknown to Jack and Don, the damage had been done. Johnny Laskowski was upset by this incident, and while it was not clear if it factored into his decision to shortly thereafter join McKenzie Air Service, it likely didn't help. What was clear was that they were still short an engineer.

The man who filled the position was Fraser "Fuzz" Henderson, despite the fact that the ink had hardly dried on his aircraft engineering licence. No matter: Mulholland needed an engineer and Fuzz needed a job, so two problems were solved. The only wrinkle was that Fuzz was deathly afraid of wolves and was about to head north into wolf country. To his credit, he managed to put aside his fear, although he had no way of knowing that he was about to get a lot closer to wolves than he had ever imagined.

Buckbrush and Busted Wings, 1937

By now it was late November of 1937, the plane's wheels had been replaced with skis, and finally they were ready to go. Don's family were all at the airport to see him off. Fuzz, Jack Mulholland, a pet cat, and the ten-gallon fuel tank were packed up front, and Don flew from the rear cockpit. Shortly before they were about to take off, a twin engine Lockheed Electra 10A on skis returned to the airport. At the controls was pilot Herbert Hollick-Kenyon, and with him was legendary explorer Sir Hubert Wilkins. They were searching for Sigmund Levanevsky, a famous Russian aviator flying a Soviet four-engine bomber with a crew of five, who had gone missing the previous August 12 on a flight from Moscow to Fairbanks, Alaska. They had returned to the airport because of deteriorating weather conditions. Don wisely decided that if these experienced men felt it wasn't fit to fly, he was in no position to second-guess them, and he scrubbed the flight.

Two days later the weather had improved, and the flight was on. The first stop was Athabasca, and the next was High Prairie on the west end of Lesser Slave Lake. On the way to Grande Prairie, they encountered heavy snow, and as a precaution, landed in a farm field near Valleyview. The farm was the property of the Doris family. There were two girls in the family, one of whom would later become Don's sister-in-law. The airplane was sharing the field with some horses and cattle, so Don

moved it onto a mound to get it out of harm's way. The next day, he could see that snow was curiously cleared from various places on the upper wing. Apparently the turkeys on the farm had been flying up to roost on the wing, and sliding down when they couldn't get a good grip. While there was no harm done, Don was concerned. "I worried about the plane the whole time."

After another two-day wait, they reached Grande Prairie, and once again were grounded by snow. People from town came out to see the airplane, and Don met the local priest, Father McQuire. They knew each other from St. Alphonsus in Edmonton, and Father McQuire

Jack Mulholland and Don Patry
standing in front of Fairchild CF-AUU.
Unidentified person in cockpit.
Photo taken prior
to crash at Patry Lake.
D.V. Patry collection

insisted that Don come and speak to his students. "Well, holy smokes, I had to go and talk to the kids. He introduced me as his altar boy, which I never was, but I used to put the new licence plates on his car every year, or if there was something wrong with his car, he'd get me to look at it or change a tire. Anyway, I was royally treated." The stay at Grande Prairie lasted about four days.

The next leg of the trip was to Fort St. John, BC, where they ran into more snow and landed about fifteen miles north of town, at the farm of a trader by the name of Joe Clark. Don flew back to Fort St. John for fuel and supplies, and stayed overnight. The next morning he had a very difficult time getting the Fairchild to start. The starting system did have an additional magneto to give extra spark to the plugs, but it had to be cranked while the engine was hand propped, an impossible task for only one man. Eventually, after considerable effort, he succeeded in getting the J65 Wright radial to fire up and was able to return to the farm.

The next day, the weather was cooperating—"It was a nice, clear day. Boy, was it beautiful."—and they got going. The destination was Fort Nelson, but they inadvertently went past it: "There was a ring around Fort Nelson on the map and I expected to see a place as big as Fort St. John. We went right by Fort Nelson; I could see the houses by the river, and I could see ski tracks on the river, but only three or four houses, so I thought, that can't be it. I had never seen Fort Nelson before, as I'd never been north of Waugh!"

Don was getting concerned about the fuel supply and decided to land on a small lake, known at that time as Sandy Lake, to add fuel from the can stowed up front. The lake is now officially called Patry Lake, named after Don, and is located about forty-five miles southeast of Nelson Forks, BC. Jack said to land close to shore, as he didn't trust the ice conditions, so they flew over and Don had a quick look, saw a point of land, and turned toward it. Now the landing was complicated by a couple of things. The first was that the Fairchild had a coupe top that originally belonged to a smaller plane, resulting in the front passengers blocking the pilot's forward view when the plane was in the landing attitude. The second was that the heater in the plane was poor, and by now Don could not feel his feet on the rudder pedals.

"We were about to land near this point and I thought I better have a look, so I kicked it sideways, and holy smoke, there was a line of trees in front of me, low stuff. So anyway, I poured the coal to it and it popped and banged and I guess the carburetor had iced up, even though I thought I had kept working it. Gosh, anyway, it wasn't gonna catch; it was too late to do anything, then all of a sudden it caught, but the trees were right there. I pulled it up over the first row of buck brush, and there were two trees in the middle of this slough and I went right between the middle of them, and you know what that does to the wings! Well, it went down on the prop, and the steam is flying like smoke, and the two guys in front can't get out until I get my part of the canopy back. So I'm tugging at that and before I can even get thinking, why, Jack had that axe real handy and whumped it through one side, and then a fist came out the other side of the coupe top, and the cat jumped out and came to the end of its string and was dangling there, and Jack just reached over with his axe and clicked the string and away went the cat!"

They were uninjured, but Don was devastated that the plane was damaged. "We got out of the plane, and he could have hit me in the head with the axe and I wouldn't have cared!"

It got dark early at that time of the year, about three o'clock, and Jack said they needed to get moving toward the trees. There was no time to dwell on the seriousness of the situation, which was a good thing, because they were in a bit of a mess. No one knew they were down, and without a radio there was no way to communicate their predicament. They had no snowshoes. Fuzz was wondering about wolves. Food consisted of a grand total of three cans of Bully Beef, three pounds of jam, a pound of butter, a bag of loose tea, and a billycan to make it in. In their favour was the fact that no one was injured, and they had reasonable winter clothing as well as an eiderdown sleeping bag. In addition, Jack was an experienced woodsman with an axe and matches, and, very importantly, the weather was relatively mild.

So, there was nothing to do but get on with it. If they were going to get out, it would be by putting one foot in front of the other until they made tracks to civilization. The trek got off to a poor start from the get-go, as they had to head through a swamp. The ice wasn't strong enough to support them, and they went through time and again, getting soaked to the hips. Once through the swamp, they walked single file, and Fuzz inadvertently provided a bit of levity: he had both hands jammed into his coat pockets for warmth and he tripped, falling face first into the snow.

Before long they had made some progress and stopped for the night, building a fire and placing spruce tree boughs on the ground and covering themselves with the sleeping bag. Evidently, the fire was a good one: Don accidentally burned the hood off his coat, and the next day his pant legs started to fall apart from the effects of the heat. Fortunately, the weather remained fair, and they walked and camped for three days until they reached the Nelson River. On the morning of the fourth day, they awoke to find the sleeping bag covered with a layer of snow.

As their approach was from the south, they were now on the east bank of the Nelson River. Here they intercepted a toboggan trail and followed it, eventually coming upon a rough cabin, where they made camp. Despite the shelter, this turned out to be the most uncomfortable night, as there was no firewood, so it was colder than sleeping in the open on spruce boughs, and the food, of course, was long gone.

The next day, they continued on the trail until they saw a tent and a log cabin. This was an Indian camp inhabited by two women and two children—the men were away hunting. The tent had been pitched on bare ground before winter, and the men entered by sliding down the snow bank that had built up around it in the months since. The women didn't speak English, but Jack was able to communicate to the older one that they were hungry. Once she understood this, she quickly went to work, pulling out a huge frying pan into which she placed a handful of lard and began heating it on a small stove in the centre of the shelter. Then she went to a corner of the tent, pulled back a rabbit-hide blanket to reveal the hindquarter of a moose, and used an axe to cut off some meat. The floor of the tent was covered in spruce boughs, and as she chopped off the meat, it landed on the boughs and collected needles, which were fried along with the meat. This made no difference to the hungry travellers, as they ate a frying pan full each. While the kindness of their host was gratefully appreciated, Don's empty stomach rebelled at so much rich food, and he had to make a quick trip outside. Later the women allowed the visitors to go into the cabin, where they found flour, sugar, and salt to make bannock, which was a little easier on the digestive system, with extra to pack for the trail.

Interestingly enough, the elder Indians did not care to use the nearby cabin, preferring the traditional tent. The cabin belonged to a son who had died, and, being superstitious, the parents wanted nothing to do with it. It was furnished, complete with a gramophone on which the children repeatedly played "Henry Made a Lady out of Lizzy," a reference to Henry Ford's first car, the Model T, known as the Tin Lizzy, and its later refinements.

Don, Jack, and Fuzz also noticed the practical dressing style of the older woman, who had three skirts layered on top of each other. Apparently, she saw no sense in throwing away a skirt that was still functional just because she got a new one. In the wilderness, function over form is just plain good sense.

Before long, the Indian men returned to camp and were able to give directions to the nearest post, which was Nelson Forks, a day's walk away. When the three men reached Nelson Forks, Jack hired two dog teams, one to take a message to Fort Nelson and one to go back to the plane. Grant McConachie's airline, United Air Transport (UAT), had a radio station at Fort Nelson operated by Chris Christianson, and from there, information on their situation would be sent to Edmonton. Until then, no one would know that they had not reached Nahanni.

Without delay, Jack, Don, Fuzz, and the Indian with the dog team set out to return to the plane. Now equipped with snowshoes, the men found the trip back somewhat easier than the walk out had been, but it was still slow going. Jack and the guide went in front of the dogs to break trail, while Don and Fuzz followed, with Don handling the dogs, a task he found a little frustrating, as the one dog was smaller than the rest of the team. When the small dog was on the outside of a bend in the trail, it was lifted completely off its feet, and the imbalance caused the carryall to upset. Each time Don attempted to right the mess, the dogs would turn around and look at him as if to say, "What did you do this time?"

It took two days to reach the lake. After a brief inspection, during which they discovered the poor cat curled up on Don's seat in the plane, frozen solid, it was obvious to Don that they could not repair the Fairchild with the materials on hand. They decided to head back to Nelson Forks, after Jack recovered the three quarts of one-hundred-proof alcohol on board.

They made the return trip in only one day, but their haste took its toll: Don developed bad leg cramps from the snowshoes and could hardly walk. What a relief to finally come around the big bend in the river and see Nelson Forks ahead. He eventually made it to a Hudson's Bay cabin where the storekeeper, Wes, had hardtack and a large hot rum waiting for him. As soon as he finished his drink, Don found a comfortable spot on the floor, collapsed into his sleeping bag, and fell asleep.

Haywire and Bindertwine

Don and Fuzz flew back to Edmonton in a Norseman piloted by Ernie Kubicek, who was flying for Grant McConachie. By this time, Fuzz had decided he'd had his fill of this adventure and went his own way. Don was in for a penny, in for a pound, and determined to retrieve the Fairchild. He took the train to Big River, Saskatchewan, with a pilot friend by the name of Doug Gordon, and bought a Puss Moth, CF-AGW, on February 21, 1938, with the last bit of the trappers' money. They flew the Moth on skis, three hours and forty-five minutes back to Edmonton, on February 22. On February 27, Don and Doug flew it to Cooking Lake and loaded up with plywood, brass nails and screws, glue, fabric dope, and food. The next day, they left for Fort St. John, where they spent the night. March first they continued, stopping at Fort Nelson for gas and then on to Nelson Forks. Here they picked up a tent, as previously arranged by Jack Mulholland. On March 2 they made it back to Patry Lake and the damaged Fairchild.

After unloading the repair materials and stowing the damaged undercarriage of the Fairchild in the Moth to be taken out for welding, Don and Doug removed the damaged wings and pulled them into the

Don stands beside patched up Fairchild CF-AUU at Patry Lake,
March 1938. To the left is the Puss Moth CF-AGW.
D.V. Patry collection

Doug Gordon and Don Patry,
photograph "Souvenir of Kandid
Kamera Snaps, Merrick Drug
Stores, Edmonton, Alta."
D.V. Patry collection

tent. When camp was set up, Don flew on to Fort Liard and then Nahanni while Doug stayed at the lake and worked on repairs.

The repairs took ingenuity and time; the damaged sections of the spars were cut out and replaced by pieces of trees cut and dimensioned on site, and secured using plywood, screws, and glue. The broken leading edge on the wing stringer was replaced with a section of a small-diameter tree. One spar was in reasonable condition, and requiring only reinforcement with plywood. The skis were patched up with tree sections, and the brackets repaired.

From March 2–23, Don was back and forth to Edmonton and Fort St. John for supplies, and to carry on the traders' business as required. The return leg of one of these flights almost ended in disaster.

Orange Trees on the Muskwa River, 1938 (Bush Pilot with an Orange Crate)

On March 17, 1938, Don loaded the Moth with supplies and headed for Patry Lake, following the Nelson River northward as usual. At Fort Nelson the Muskwa River joins the Nelson, but Don mistakenly continued along the Muskwa. After a while, Don realized that the terrain was unfamiliar and to make matters worse, the engine oil pressure had dropped dangerously low due to lack of oil. He decided he had no choice but to land on the frozen river below to add more oil. The landing was routine and the oil was quickly topped up. Then the trouble started. The snow was deep, and Don had to tramp a runway for takeoff. Even then, the Moth needed a push to break the skis free of the snow. Another tough job for a man flying alone, but riskier this time—if he pushed hard enough to free the skis, the plane could take off without him. The solution was low tech, and might work: Don tied one end of a string to the throttle, and the other around his wrist. Theoretically, if the Moth started to get away with Don on the ground, the tightening string would pull the throttle back to idle and give Don a chance to jump aboard.

On the first attempt at takeoff, the tramped runway ran out before the Moth got airborne. Since Don couldn't turn the plane around, it was back to square one: more tramping, followed by another takeoff attempt with the same result. The situation had progressed from routine to annoying to serious. By now the plane was some distance along the river, and the valley narrowed greatly ahead. Don decided he had to lighten the load to get the Moth airborne before he ran out of valley. He chose to jettison the cargo's highly prized crates of oranges and eggs—if there's an orange tree growing along the Muskwa River, that's how it got there!

The reduction in weight did the trick, and the skis broke free of the snow. With no room to turn, the question was whether the Moth could out-climb the valley walls. Don coaxed the best angle of climb that he dared as the sides got closer and closer. He finally banked and added some opposite rudder to clear the opening on an angle, since he wasn't positive he would get through with wings level. He made it.

Free of the Muskwa, Don climbed for altitude at full throttle. While he had escaped the Muskwa, he still didn't know exactly where he was. Lost would not be the correct description: he knew where he had started from and where he wanted to go, it was just the in-between part that required some immediate sorting out. Before long he was high enough to get a look around. The visibility was good, and sure enough, he was able to spot the lake. With some relief, he pointed the nose toward the lake and pondered how he would break the news to Doug that there would be no scrambled eggs or orange juice for breakfast.

In short order, Don was back on the lake, safely landed and shut down. Entering the tent, he was taken aback by the reception he got. Doug was crouching over a blowpot, heating dope to apply to the fabric repairs. Not hearing Don arrive, he was greatly startled when he realized someone or something was in the tent with him. He turned suddenly to face the entrance, and what a sight he was: unshaven, hair matted to his head, grasping what had once been a brush but was now only bristles. Don didn't know if he should laugh or run. Once he had recovered from his surprise, Doug explained that he'd had a little accident with the highly flammable dope and the blowpot that resulted in a small fire, some big excitement, and the handle burned off the one and only brush.

Before long the Fairchild was reassembled and more or less ready for a test flight. When Don and Doug got the engine running, it vibrated excessively due to the damage to the metal prop during the landing, not to mention Jack Mulholland's attempt to straighten it with his axe. The prop was adjustable from the ground, and Don was able to get it set so that the vibration was only noticeable at particular throttle settings. On

Norseman CF-BFR as RCAF aircraft No. 696.
Impressed into RCAF service February 1940.
Western Canada Aviation Museum

the first test flight, one wing flew low and they made a hard landing on the lake, well away from any trees. Don adjusted the flying wires to change the angle of the wing, and cured the problem.

A Norseman Mark IV, CF-BFR, flew over the lake and Don recognized it as Grant McConachie's. McConachie's engineer was "Toomer" Taylor, and Don thought it would be worthwhile to get his opinion on the make-do repairs, so he and Doug piled into the Moth and hopped over to Nelson Forks, where Grant had a base. Here they did indeed meet up with Grant and his engineer, and eventually concluded that it would be reasonable to fly the Fairchild out. No details on the rest of the evening's activities are known, but Grant liked to socialize and no doubt they all enjoyed the visit.

The next morning, Don and Doug were up early and on the river, tramping a runway in the snow for the Moth. The first takeoff attempt came to a stop in the snow, and it was back to tramping. In the meantime, Grant was up and about, and had fired up the Norseman. What happened next could be best described as a mix of showmanship, competitiveness, risk, and ego, with a dash of hellery thrown in for good measure—in other words, typical McConachie. In front of his guests, Grant firewalled the throttle, plowed through the snow, lifted off, and waggled his wings in greeting on the way past. Salutations may have been shouted in return, but you can bet it wasn't, "Good morning, Grant!"

Fairchild CF-AUU flown by Don Patry, D.H. Puss Moth CF-AGW flown by Doug Gordon, Norseman Mark IV CF-BFR flown by Grant McConachie, Charlie Lake, Fort St. John BC, March 1938 . The Fairchild had been repaired after being damaged at Patry Lake. Although flyable, the DOT inspector grounded AUU and it never flew again.
D.V. Patry collection

Once back at the lake, they got things packed up, and on March 23, 1938, they left for the last time, Don in the Fairchild and Doug in the Moth. They landed at Fort Nelson for fuel and then departed for Charlie Lake, Fort St. John. Two hours and forty minutes later, they made Charlie Lake safely; however, the plan to continue on to Edmonton was derailed by a Department of Transport inspector named Jock Currie, who intercepted Don at Charlie Lake to tell him that the Fairchild would not fly until it was made airworthy. In fact, he wanted to know what the hell Don thought he was doing flying it at all. Don explained what had happened, and emphasized that he had consulted with an engineer about the temporary repairs. This more or less placated Currie, as he decided not to write Don up on airworthiness infractions; however, the Fairchild was still grounded. So now the Fairchild had to be dismantled once again, loaded onto a truck, belonging to Red Powell, and transported to Dawson Creek, crossing the frozen Peace River on the way. At Dawson Creek, the plane was put on a train to Edmonton. Doug stayed at Charlie Lake to look after the Fairchild, and Don went on with the Moth.

Don headed south and stayed overnight north of Grande Prairie at Bear Lake. The lake was frozen, with open water near the shore. The next morning the Moth was difficult to start, because with a broken blowpot, Don could not preheat it. The engine finally caught, however, and he flew on to Cooking Lake. Here he replaced the skis with wheels, and flew the final leg to Edmonton.

Trappers' Luck Runs Out

With the Fairchild dealt with for the time being, Jack Mulholland wanted to get trapping before the season was a complete loss, so on April 15, 1938, he had Don fly him, along with two dogs, to a small lake in the Nahanni region, Northwest Territories. Don made a second trip the same day to bring in another trapper, Ollie Law. The plan was for Don to return to retrieve them later in the spring, with the Fairchild on floats. It was not to be.

Don flew the Moth to Prince Albert, Saskatoon, and Calgary, trying to arrange for repair work on AUU. However, no one, perhaps wisely considering the economy at the time, would consider repairing it without cash up front, and there was no cash. After what it had taken to get the plane out of the bush and back to Edmonton, this was a bitter pill for Don to swallow. Returning from Calgary on April 24, Don ran into a snowstorm and had to spend the night in Carstairs. The next day's flight to Edmonton turned out to be Don's last in the Moth. The trappers' grubstake and luck had run out. There was no money to fuel the Moth, and AUU was still in pieces.

Things had not changed by the time the ice was out of the rivers, and Don was getting messages, each one more urgent than the last, from Jack's wife, Daisy, asking when he was going back in to pick up Jack. Finally, Don went to the police to report the trappers' plight. McKenzie Air Service was sent in to look for the trappers, but they had already abandoned camp.

Jack and Ollie reached Fort Simpson by raft on July 4, 1938, after floating down an unnamed river that emptied into Great Slave Lake. The trip out was a little rough, even by trappers' standards. The food had run out, and they had been forced to eat the dogs or starve. All the furs had been lost in various upsets in rapids. To add insult to injury, Jack's creditor, Theodore Bartsch, claimed on his security. Unfortunately for Jack, most of what he owned had been pledged against a fifteen-hundred-dollar loan. By Jack's estimate, property and goods worth $5,720 were seized, putting him out of business.

Eventually, both the Moth and the Fairchild came to inglorious ends as well. The Moth was left out behind a hangar at Edmonton to be cannibalized for parts. The Fairchild ended up at a tech school in Calgary, where greenhorn engineers could learn the ropes by eagerly taking it apart and rebuilding with no cash upfront required.

In April 1938, Don had returned to flying for the weatherman at Edmonton in the flying club's Fleet Finch and Gypsy Moth, and doing a little barnstorming in his Cirrus Moth G-CAUE along with Doug Gordon and Jack Ross in Doug's Waco 10 three-seater CF-HUU. Jack was a flying instructor in Edmonton. They'd land near the outskirts of Alberta towns and hop rides at two dollars for the curious folks who would come out to have a look at the airplanes. Pilots in the area had done this kind of informal flying for years. As a matter of fact, in the fall of 1931, before Don had even touched a prop, a plane had landed in a field on the edge of Killam, Alberta, near the town school, causing the day's lesson to be halted as the children and teacher rushed outside to see the excitement. One adventuresome young girl ran home (through the stubble fields, ruining her silk stockings) to raid her piggybank to pay for her first flight. Thrilled with her first taste of flying, little did she know at the time that aviation would play a major role in the rest of her life. That young aviatrix was Irene Carson, Don's future bride.

Final Flight of AUE

Around June of 1938, Don and Frank Burton sold the Moth AUE to a couple of characters who had a farm near Grimshaw, Alberta. After the transaction was completed, Don delivered AUE to the eager new owners.

"I took it up and landed in a field. I can't remember their names, but I do recall that the one fella had a glass eye, and I told them to taxi it around a bit to get a feel for the plane before they flew it. But they maintained that they had flown a lot of airplanes. Anyway, it turns out that I had no sooner left and they decided they'd taxi around the field. The guy with one eye gets in the plane and starts taxiing around, and his partner decides that he wants to get in the back with his own control stick. So, as he's trying to catch up to the airplane, "One Eye" opens the throttle a little bit and the closer the guy gets, the more power he adds. Well, the first thing he knows, One Eye looks out and he's off the ground, headed right for the town of Grimshaw!

"Luckily there was a row of trees right before town and this guy, not knowing what to do, twiddled the stick over to the side and rolled right into them. When the dust settled, here if he didn't crawl out of the wreck unhurt except for a cut right through his cheek. He was half-tanked, I guess, and he stuck his tongue out through the hole and thought it was a great joke! They took him to the hospital and that's the last I ever heard about it. I don't think they ever got that airplane flying again. We were up to the Peace River a few years ago and I wanted to talk to those guys, but I couldn't find hide nor hair of either one of them. That was a long, long time ago, and I guess that was the end of UE."

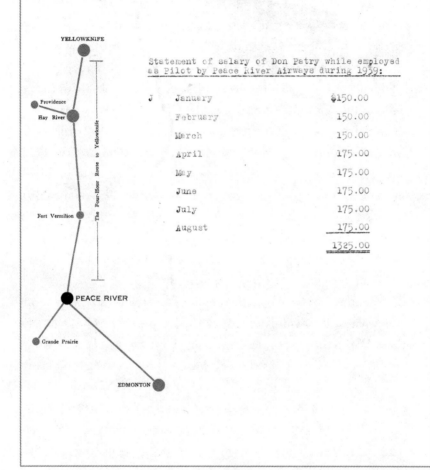

Peace River Airways Limited

Peace River

ALBERTA

YELLOWKNIFE

Providence
Hay River

Fort Vermilion

The Four-Hour Route to Yellowknife

PEACE RIVER

Grande Prairie

EDMONTON

Statement of salary of Don Patry while employed
as Pilot by Peace River Airways during 1939:

J	January	$150.00
	February	150.00
	March	150.00
	April	175.00
	May	175.00
	June	175.00
	July	175.00
	August	175.00
		1325.00

Salary statement from Peace River Airways showing Don's salary for 1939.
D.V. Patry collection

CHAPTER TWO: **PEACE RIVER AIRWAYS**

Dal Dalziel

In July 1938, Don was contacted by thirty-year-old George "Dal" Dalziel, chief and only pilot of the newly formed Peace River Airways (PRA), with an offer to fly a Fokker on floats. Don jumped at the chance. Dalziel was a hard-living, colourful character, a combination of pilot, trapper, entrepreneur, and adventurer. Dalziel was also the only pilot ever to have his plane attacked by a bear. He flew a Curtis Robin, a three-passenger plane, and on one trip, while the plane was moored on the Nahanni riverbank, a bear tore the side of the plane to shreds to get at a slab of bacon inside. Using skins he had just trapped, Dal patched the fuselage and flew home to Fort Simpson. Today that airplane is in the Reynolds-Alberta Museum in Westaskiwin, Alberta.

The episode with the bear aside, Dalziel was no fool, as he demonstrated with his involvement in the formation of Peace River Airways. A group of businessmen and professionals, including a doctor, a dentist, a lawyer, a farmer, and a storekeeper, had joined together in 1938 to create this new airline. They were Jack McNeill, Dr. H. Fish, Leon Giroux, Dr. H. Murray, W.R. Little, Ernie Kubicek, Mrs. Nora Cowan, E. McAdams, and Dave Koelin. Shares were twenty-five dollars each. The plan was to generate revenue by flying fresh farm produce and supplies from the Peace River country to Yellowknife in float-equipped Wacos. Dalziel put twenty-five hundred dollars into the company, and convinced the investors to buy his five-place Fokker Universal G-CAHE as well as another Fokker G-CAHJ from Grant McConachie's Yukon Southern Air Transport (YSAT), rather than the Wacos.

As he had not flown this type of aircraft before, Don needed some training, which consisted of crouching behind the single seat while Dalziel flew a circuit. The post-flight review was succinct. Dalziel: "See how it's done?" Patry: "I guess so." Don then took HE for a quick

Peace River Airways Fokker Universal G-CAHJ, at Fort Vermillin, Alberta.
The plane Don flew for his first "airline" job.
D.V. Patry collection

circuit and back to the dock to be loaded. Dal took off in HJ and Don followed in HE. Once en route, Dal pulled back the coupe top and, to Don's amusement, stood up and looked around to confirm that Don was following. Dal found the coupe top convenient for regular jettisons: the cockpit's storage space was just the right size for a case of beer, which explained the empty bottles flying out of HJ in-flight!

The first leg of the flight was to Peace River, and a lot of people came down to the dock to see the new airline. After a quick lunch, it was on to Fort Vermilion, where Don happened to meet the wife of a doctor he knew from Edmonton. Their conversation was a little one-sided, because after flying all day with no hearing protection, Don could not hear a thing. The next day, Dalziel was up early and they flew to Hay River and then to Yellowknife. At the start of the next leg, Don was unable to get his heavily loaded plane off the water, so Dalziel decided to help out and try to get HE airborne himself. Sure enough, his piloting skills came through and away they went. However, it wasn't long into the trip that Dalziel realized he had made a major error: he was in HE but his beer was in HJ. By the time the first leg was completed, his tongue was hanging out!

Repair and Fly, or Stay and Die

In the fall of 1938, Don was flying a party of four from Yellowknife to Fort Vermilion when engine trouble caused a forced landing and an unplanned camp-out. On board were summer engineering students Thomas Senior and Kendall Kidder, as well as miners Norm Blatchford and Eric Larson. Smoke from forest fires had reduced visibility, and Don could not climb high enough to clear the thirty-five-hundred-foot Caribou Hills between Hay River and Fort Vermilion. Instead he tried to skirt the Hills to the west side, but suddenly the engine dropped a valve and lost power. Don's low-keyed version of the event is that he then proceeded to put down on a small lake. While factually accurate, this description doesn't do justice to the situation, which had all the ingredients for a disaster: a fully loaded plane flying at low altitude in poor visibility with engine problems. With no time to spare, through the haze Don spotted a lake that looked big enough to land on, and down they went. After the landing, it was obvious the lake was little more than a small slough. But they and the plane were down safely, and that muddy slough looked magnificent. However, they were far from out of the woods yet.

Don had earned his air engineer certificate earlier in the year, writing the DOT Aircraft Engineers exams in Edmonton for a week. While he had not participated in a formal engineering apprenticeship, he had so much practical experience that the accreditation was justly awarded. As a teenager, he had worked as an apprentice mechanic under the supervision of a neighbour, Jim Coles, who was a licenced auto mechanic. He also worked in his older brother's garage and had taken his own Model T apart so many times he could do it blindfolded. Now he was in a situation that made his exams look like a walk in the park. If he couldn't get the plane's engine repaired, they would have to wait until someone found them, or try to walk out. Either option was a long shot at best.

After getting a shore camp set up, Don started work on the engine and removed the bottom cylinder. He then discovered that the collett ring had broken off the intake valve, causing the valve to stick open and lose both compression and power. As well, one of the intake manifold tubes had a hole in it, causing even more power to be lost. Don found a metal file in the small collection of tools on board, and began the arduous task of filing out a new groove around the damaged valve stem. This was slow, tedious work and just possible on the intake valve—it would have been completely impossible on the hardened exhaust valves. The brass valve guide also had to be filed down to accommodate the shortened valve stem. After three days, the engine was back together and running, but the slough was as short as before. Playing it safe, Don went solo. Just as brakes would be used for a short field takeoff, he roped the plane to a tree to get the engine rpm up before the plane started to move and lost valuable takeoff distance. At maximum rpm, he released the rope, and took off successfully.

Meanwhile, a pilot named Jack Moore was searching for the missing party in a Junkers, but couldn't locate them in such a large area. Don made Fort Vermilion without incident, reported what had happened, and had the engine repaired. Dal Dalziel flew a food-drop to the lake, not wanting to chance a landing. Two days later, after replacing the offending cylinder, Don was back to pick up his passengers. He flew them out one at a time to a larger lake about fifteen minutes away, and then took the group to Fort Vermilion. On the way, someone produced a bottle of rum, and a little in-flight celebration ensued, which turned out to more of a hardship than being stranded in the wild; by the time they reached the Peace River at Fort Vermilion, one of the students was as sick as a dog. As well, one of the miners was concentrating on his song and his cigar, and he stepped off the float straight into the river, missing the dock completely. He bobbed to the surface and was fished out, with water pouring out of his vest and his cigar clamped firmly between his teeth.

An Act of God
Another memorable flight from Yellowknife occurred around Christmas 1938, with the temperature dipping to sixty below. The destination was

Peace River and there were four passengers in the Waco CF-BJS, three guys in the rear and one up front. The fellow in the front, Bert Nieland, would later make a name for himself by pioneering the first Cat train from Grimshaw to Yellowknife, using bulldozers to haul goods over the frozen lakes and bush.

It was very cold during the flight, and at the end of Great Slave Lake at Lower Hay River, Don decided to land to get warmed up. Immediately, they were greeted by the resident Anglican minister, Reverend Richards, who came running out to the plane. He was clearly agitated and exclaimed, "It was an act of God that you landed!" It turned out that his wife was in desperate need of medical attention, with complications resulting from pregnancy. Under these circumstances, the sudden unscheduled appearance of a plane really was a miracle. Two of the passengers were single guys in no hurry to get home, and they volunteered to stay over so that Mrs. Richards and a nurse from Hay River, Ms. Neville, could fly out. They bundled Mrs. Richards into the rear of the plane in Don's goose down sleeping bag, along with the nurse, and then quickly departed, right into a low-pressure system and the bad weather that went with it.

The visibility was not good to start with, and was made worse by frost buildup on the inside of the windshield. To make matters even more interesting, carburetor ice, reducing engine performance, was a constant problem. The only way Don could clear the ice was to turn the ignition off and on in flight. This caused a bit of popping and backfiring from the engine, and was very disconcerting for the passengers. Bert Neiland's job was to keep the windshield clear so Don could follow the river, bend by bend, all the way to Fort Vermilion. Things were a little tense, and Bert was feeling it: he'd clear the frost, look back at the suffering Mrs. Richards, and then, white-faced, scrape even faster. In any event, he held up his end, and Don made a safe landing on the river, although the engine quit while taxiing because of the carb ice.

In short order, a cutter drawn by two horses appeared and navigated the winding trail down to the river to meet them. Another act of God:

the fellow in the cutter had simply heard them fly over and land, and came to see what was going on. After some hurried explanations, the patient and nurse were transferred to the cutter and started off.

No one could have foreseen what happened next, nor could they have considered it an act of God; when Don restarted the engine, the noise spooked the horses and they bolted, throwing the driver out. Everyone watched in disbelief as the runaway cutter tore around the first bend, somehow staying upright. On the second turn, it climbed the bank and tipped, spilling the two women into the snow. Thankfully, neither was injured, but at the same time, it didn't do either of them, particularly Mrs. Richards, any good. Eventually, she was hospitalized in Hamilton, Ontario. Don never heard how things turned out. However, twenty-nine years later, in 1967, he attended a tribute to bush pilots in Yellowknife, and as luck would have it, met Nurse Neville from the mercy flight. When he asked her if she remembered him, she replied, "Oh God, you're that young fellow! I've always wondered where on earth he got to!"

Waco CF-BJS on a sand bar at Peace River for change over to wheels, spring 1938.
D.V. Patry collection

Adventure with Reverend Richards and Chief Stubby

After Mrs. Richards' evacuation episode, Don would often be hosted by the Reverend when he was overnight at Lower Hay. On one occasion, a message came that an Indian child was gravely ill, so Don and Reverend Richards set out to find the camp on Wood Lake, about twenty miles southeast of Hay River. The directions were a little vague and they were unable to spot the tiny settlement in the bush. They did, however, see another encampment and decided to set down.

The landing site looked ideal, a smooth, snow-covered open area with trees on each side. However, on final approach, the white featureless surface made it impossible to judge the height of the plane above the frozen river, and Don decided to go around rather than chance a risky landing. Fortunately, the engine responded to the application of throttle and the Fokker G-CAHE climbed to safety. They landed out on the river and taxied back.

The local chief, known as Chief Stubby, had harnessed his dog team when he heard the plane fly over and was waiting for them when they got in. Don and the Reverend got in the carryall and they headed for camp. The temperature was well below zero, and Don never forgot the dramatic sight of the chief urging the dogs on, with his face and parka covered with frost.

They soon reached the chief's house, a snug one-room log cabin. In short order, a double team of dogs was organized, and one of the men from the camp set out with the Reverend to find the ailing boy. Don stayed with the chief, who was insistent that he be given something for his troubles. This put Don in a predicament, until he thought to give the chief a religious statue of Our Lady of Fatima that he happened to have in his jacket. This greatly pleased the chief, and got Don back in his favour.

The next morning, Don and the chief left in the plane to find the other camp. The chief was supposed to be navigating. "As soon as we got airborne, he was lost, but I had an idea of where to go and we found the place and landed." The news that greeted them was not good: the boy had died during the night, a victim of illness and isolation. It was a sombre trip back to Hay River.

The Winter Cat Train—Mile 0 to Yellowknife

In the winter of 1940–41, an incredible transportation feat through the frozen bush from Grimshaw to Yellowknife was accomplished. The concept was simple: haul sleds of food and supplies northward during the winter, using the extremely cold temperatures to advantage as the bogs and rivers freeze into roads. The innovation was in using bulldozers, or Cats, rather than dog teams. The Cats pulled a train of large wooden sleds, hence the name cat train. While simple in concept, the logistics of this project were daunting. The principal organizers were Bert Nieland and Neil Harcourt. Bert was a hands-on sort, while Neil was a business manager.

"The cat train was instigated in the summer. They built all the sleds and then got supplies ready to take up to Yellowknife. The winter trail branched off into Fort Vermilion and Carcajou and a couple other places, and then it went up to Upper Hay. They crossed over the river just above Upper Hay and went down the west side, and crossed over below some falls, and then went down the east side of the river right into the town of Hay River. The idea was to service all these communities during the winter, hauling stuff like fuel instead of going down the river and way around by steamboat. It was a much shorter run to go cross country.

"I flew this Neil fellow from Peace River up to Fort Vermilion to show him what the old winter trail was like. After that he went by dog team and checked it out, and got a few guides around Fort St. John that had horse teams to travel the winter road into Fort Nelson.

"I also flew him to some farms around Fort Vermilion in the old Fokker on skis. The Mennonite farmers there raised cattle and he'd buy from them, and they would butcher the cattle and haul the meat over to Fort Vermilion. When the train came in, meat and other supplies were loaded. We sort of followed the train from the air on our trips

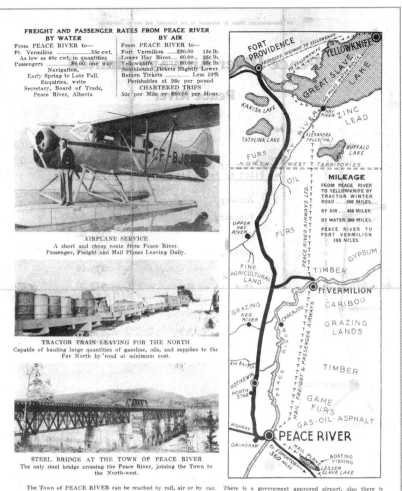

FREIGHT AND PASSENGER RATES FROM PEACE RIVER

BY WATER	BY AIR
From PEACE RIVER to—	From PEACE RIVER to—
Ft. Vermilion ....55c cwt.	Fort Vermilion ......$30.00 15c lb.
As low as 40c cwt. in quantities	Lower Hay River.... 60.00 25c lb.
Passengers ....$6.00 one way	Yellowknife .... 80.00 38c lb.
Navigation,	Southbound Tickets Slightly Lower.
Early Spring to Late Fall.	Return Tickets .... Less 10%
Enquiries, write	Perishables at 26c per pound
Secretary, Board of Trade,	CHARTERED TRIPS
Peace River, Alberta	50c per Mile or $50.00 per Hour.

AIRPLANE SERVICE
A short and cheap route from Peace River.
Passenger, Freight and Mail Planes Leaving Daily.

TRACTOR TRAIN LEAVING FOR THE NORTH
Capable of hauling large quantities of gasoline, oils, and supplies to the
Far North by road at minimum cost.

STEEL BRIDGE AT THE TOWN OF PEACE RIVER
The only steel bridge crossing the Peace River, joining the Town to
the North-west.

MILEAGE
FROM PEACE RIVER
TO YELLOWKNIFE BY
TRACTOR WINTER
ROAD .... 500 MILES.
BY AIR . . . 450 MILES.
BY WATER 940 MILES.
PEACE RIVER TO
FORT VERMILION
300 MILES.

The Town of PEACE RIVER can be reached by rail, air or by car. There is a government approved airport, also there is suitable landing facilities on water when pontoons are in use by planes.

When the river permits, freight and passenger boat service runs regularly between Peace River and Fort Vermilion. The Town is also served by the Northern Alberta Railways, who give first-class passenger and freight service from Edmonton to Peace River overnight.

Peace River Town is modern in every way with hotels, cafes and stores, also creamery, flour mill and packing plant. The latter two are using the natural gas facilities which are available. The town itself is recognized as a wholesale centre.

Promotional brochure for Peace River Airways.
D.V. Patry collection

to Yellowknife. It wasn't exactly on our route, but we'd sashay over to where the trail was just to see how they were doing.

"It was a real success, but I don't know what happened to that train. I did hear that Bert was drowned coming back in the spring when his Cat went through the ice. I'm not sure of that, but that's what I heard."

Cat Tracks

"In the spring, before the train left Yellowknife to cross the lake, we had a soft spell and the old Cats, they made a great big wide track mark in the snow, and it melted a little bit and then froze over. I was in to Hay River with the old Fokker and had to stay overnight. The next morning, I got going and I cut across this track at about a forty-five degree angle, and the outside ski, my left-hand ski, it followed the rut and it twisted the undercart off, and down I went on one wing. It broke it right off at the fitting on the fuselage at the top where the leg went up.

"There was an old Anglican mission there and they had lots of stuff around, and I was able to get a hold of some pipes and flatten them out, and make a plate to go over the fuselage and down over the leg. I had to drill holes by hand and use just ordinary bolts that I could scrounge from the mission. Anyway, I got it hooked together, and I flew it out and got it back to Fort McClennan in Alberta. That winter we were parked on a little lake just south of Peace River, about halfway between Grande Prairie and Peace River. Frank Burton was the mechanic at that time, and he welded the gear back together.

"A couple of trips later, after flying into Yellowknife, I came back to Hay River, and the minute I hit Hay River it started to snow. I was following the darned river back up to Upper Hay to find the winter road across from Upper Hay back into Fort Vermilion. In the snow I followed every bloody little bend in that river, and when I got into Upper Hay, I was so tired I just got out of the airplane and left it. I usually put poles or something under the skis so they wouldn't freeze down, but I was exhausted and not thinking ahead. Anyway, in the morning when I started the engine to go home, I was stuck.

"It was Easter and there was a priest saying mass in a log cabin there when I started the engine. I was getting the tail up and kicking the rudder around, but it wouldn't move. A bunch of local Indians come along and they were all watching, and then they all got on one side and started to push and they just twisted off that leg that I'd broke before. So down on one wing again. You know, I guess I'm slated for hell or something, because the poor priest, he'd say a bit of mass, then he'd come and help me, and then he'd go back in for a little while, and come out again.

"So it was the same old thing. I happened to get some old sleigh runners, long and about two inches wide. The Indians used them to make their carryalls. I patched the thing up the same as I did before and got it out. It was put on floats after that and I don't know if it ever got fixed properly. I've often thought of that poor priest. I should have just left everything and gone to mass with the guy!"

Red Hot Flying
"One trip from Yellowknife, I got back to Fort Vermilion and the old engine dropped part of a tappet, but I was able to keep going. I was landing at a little strip at McLennan, about twenty-five minutes south of Peace River. I had never flown that airplane at night before, and it got dark. Well, the little short exhaust stack was blasting flame right out on to the fuselage and I thought, holy smokes, the airplane's gonna catch fire! But we had been flying it like that all along; I'd just never seen it before."

The End of PRA
Dalziel had gone east to the Lakehead, now known as Thunder Bay, and bought a Waco CF-BJS on credit, but 1938 was a bad year for forest fires. Peace River Airways was hit hard. The smoke was often so bad that flights had to be cancelled or aborted partway. This meant that fresh produce soon spoiled, and losses mounted. On the positive side, Peace

River Airways was granted a licence to deliver liquor to Yellowknife. Customers would prepay their order and get delivery in the next trip or two. This system worked well until Don started getting complaints from Yellowknife that people had paid but not received their order. A little investigating first revealed an empty carton in the back of Dal's plane, and then that Dal had a business on the side of making unscheduled landings and selling liquor to the Native people. As a result, he and Peace River Airways parted company. Short a pilot, Don talked Frank Burton into coming up to Peace River. However, Frank's talent was more as an engineer than a pilot, and before long, Ernie Kubicek joined Peace River Airways as pilot and investor. Unfortunately, the business side of things went from bad to worse, and Peace River Airways folded the tent. The last time Don saw HJ, it was hauled up on the riverbank at Peace River to await an unknown fate.

As it turned out, it wasn't just the equipment that bore the brunt of PRA's financial difficulties. When Don was flying, he "lived off the company" inasmuch as his accommodations and meals were either free, courtesy of hospitable locals, or charged to Peace River Airways. His

Waco CF-BJS on floats, Yellowknife 1938, Don is third from the left.
This plane is being rebuilt after fifty years in the bush.
D.V. Patry collection

personal expenses were modest, so he had no need for a lot of cash, and the fact that he wasn't getting a regular paycheque was not a big concern, given the mutual understanding that eventually the company would settle up back wages with the pilots. What he had no way of knowing was that someone inside the company was cooking the books. According to the payroll records, he had been paid in full, despite never seeing a penny. To add insult to injury, the taxman demanded his cut, sending Don a bill for five hundred dollars! Regardless of the injustice, Don paid the tax bill.

As for Dal, he eventually found financial success as a trapper, and in 1950 he launched a three-plane bush flying airline, BC-Yukon Air Services. He died on December 26, 1982, of a stroke, at Saltspring Island, BC, according to the January 17, 1983 issue of *Alberta Report*.

CHAPTER THREE: ADVENTURES IN AIRLINE TRANSPORT

McConachie's Outfit

In 1939, Don decided that if he was going to have a future in aviation, he needed to be licenced as an Airline Transport Pilot (ATP). The stumbling block was the cost: if he wanted this endorsement, he would have to pay the freight himself. The trouble was, while Don had been doing lots of flying, PRA had done little paying and he was basically broke. His financial situation was not unique, given that this was the tail end of the depression and many others were in the same boat. Looking back, Don realized that this was a critical turning point in his life: his flying career could easily have stalled right then and there if it hadn't been for a mink rancher by the name of Geoffrey T. "Jeff" Webb.

Jeff was a friend of Don's older brothers, and had a mink farm near Edmonton. He must have been a good business manager, since he was in a position to loan Don the significant sum of two hundred dollars to finance his training. Don sold his Cirrus Moth AUE to repay the debt. Jeff became a transport pilot himself, and on October 8, 1957, he made headlines in the *Edmonton Journal* when he survived the crash of an Eldorado Aviation DC-3 while flying as first officer for Captain William "Tiny" Ferris. Ice forced the plane down about fifty miles north of Fort McMurray. Tiny broke both ankles, and Jeff was badly cut on his hands and face. Sheltering themselves in the wreck, they survived a blizzard and were rescued after three days, a little the worse for wear. When asked if he would fly again, Tiny stoically replied from his hospital bed, "Well, you've got to eat."

The ATP instructor was Maurice Burbidge, who also had been Don's first instructor. "I took the course in Edmonton. We had to fly around under the hood in a Fleet Finch. There was about four of us got our transport licence together in the spring of 1939. Most of the time, we flew with one another as safety pilot."

It was a memorable moment when Don received his new licence in the mail. "I was back at PRA, and there was a man and wife working there, writing stories about the company. They lived in the hotel where I was staying. When I got that licence, I roared over and showed it to them!"

Shortly thereafter, Don let it be known to Bob Johnson, the station agent at Peace River for Grant McConachie's United Air Transport (UAT), that he was available for hire and had him forward a letter to McConachie. In time, Grant replied that he'd fly up to the grass strip at Peace River to meet Don, which he did in a Fokker Universal Standard, call sign G-CAFU. (This was the first Fokker to fly in Canada; it was imported from New York by Western Canada Airways in late 1926, flown by Harold Anthony "Doc" Oaks.) Grant would already have formed an opinion on Don's flying abilities, as they had crossed paths before and by now Don had a reputation as a good pilot who didn't rattle easily. This would explain the rather nonchalant approach that Grant took to giving Don a checkout: he simply told him that he would be flying to Grande Prairie, and then disappeared into the rear of the plane.

One of Grant McConachie's first planes, Fokker Universal Standard G-CAFU.
Red Lake Museum Photo Gallery

Left to right, CF-BMW Barkley Grow, Fairchild FC2W2, CF-ABM
Fairchild 71, CF-BDL Waco Custom, Charlie Lake, Fort St. John, BC.
Planes belonging to Grant McConachie's Yukon Southern Air Transport.
D.V. Patry collection

The Fokker was a little challenging on the ground, as it had no brakes and no steerable tailwheel. Shortly into the flight, the door to the rear compartment opened and Grant handed Don a note. With amusement, Don saw that it was a query—Grant was asking for pipe tobacco. He passed a pouch back; the door closed, and remained closed for the rest of the flight. At Grande Prairie, Grant got out and departed, flying a Barkley Grow, and Don continued to Dawson Creek to deliver some mail. Don was now flying for United Air Transport, which eventually became Yukon Southern Air Transport, and then Canadian Pacific Airways.

Ted Field was the chief pilot, and Sheldon Luck, who had quite a flying career himself—as documented in Ted Beaudoin's *Walking on Air*—was also flying for McConachie. Yukon Southern paid Don one hundred and twenty-five dollars per month. "I think I was one of the few guys that actually got money from Grant. Ted Field managed the company; he ran things. Grant would go away on one of his frequent business trips and Ted would take over and get everything going straight, and then Grant would come home and screw it all up again!"

There were no airports between Fort St. John and Whitehorse at this time, and Don was assigned the job of transporting 30-horsepower John Deere tractors to Fort Nelson and Watson Lake, to be used to build runways. He flew CF-BMW, a twin engine Barkley Grow on floats. A fellow by the name of Craig at Fort Nelson hired Indians to cut trees, and at Watson Lake Jack Baker did the same. At Charlie Lake, Red Powell rolled the ice runway with his two-ton stake truck. These were the humble beginnings of these airports.

Sandbars were also utilized as landing strips. Ted Field, Harvey Johnston, and Gord Stock of UAT would mark them with black flags and then take aerial photos that the pilots would use as reference to find them again.

After the airports were started, roads followed. "There was an old winter road from Fort St. John to Fort Nelson, but there was nothing between Nelson and Watson Lake. I flew the American engineers and they picked out a route from the air. Then they hired Indians, trappers, traders, and big-game guides. In the winter they used dog teams and in the summer pack horses, and they carried these engineers and they mapped out the Alaska Highway. They started at Dawson Creek, mile one, in 1940."

Later, when the Americans entered the Second World War, they developed the airports. "After Grant had sort of set the wheels in motion, the Americans took over. It just sort of fell in line, because that was the route they took to go up there. They built the highway and they finished the airports and then all the navigation equipment started going in, like the range stations. I flew the Canadian Department of Transport people from Nelson to Watson Lake to show them where I thought the range stations should be. But they put 'em where they wanted to. Whitehorse had a range station, and they put one in halfway between Nelson and Watson Lake at Smith River and built an airport there."

The Gutless Waco

"I was flying the Waco, CF-BDL from St. John down to Prince George to put it on floats. It was a five-place airplane, two front seats with a switch-over wheel control and a three-place bench seat in the back. They called it a freighter, because the back seat could be removed and it had a heavy-duty floor; you could get three forty-five gallon drums in there.

"It was in the spring and the rivers had opened up, so I needed to get the floats on. I landed at a little sod strip at Old Fort George beside this narrow little road that went down to the Fraser River. We put the tail up on the rack of a Yukon Southern half-ton, and the engineer, Pete Siemens, drove the truck and towed the plane. The road had been cut through hills in places, and one of the guys helping, Roy Doris, was running from one side of the bank to the other, watching the wingtips. It just sort of scraped through."

At the river, they had made a tripod out of three logs and hooked up a block and tackle. They lifted the plane with the block and tackle, took off the wheels, and slid the floats in. "It was a gutless airplane, old BDL. It took me most of the river to get the darn thing off. Pretty near wound up at Quesnel. Then I went over to Fort St. James for the mail run.

"At St. James, it was a calm day and I had a heck of a time getting off the lake. It was rigged wrong with the floats. The minute you pulled the nose up, the heels dug in and slowed the airplane. The angle of incidence of the wing was too straight—with the nose down, you would get anti-lift. It took a little while to find out that you had to get it up on the step, and then use the ailerons to wheel it over on one float and then yank it off."

Radio Communications

Learning on the job was a common theme in Don's career. Sitting in a classroom, learning theory, was of little use to a busy bush pilot. It was learn as you go, and the more practical the better. The radio was a prime example. On one occasion, Don was flying the Waco from Fort Nelson to Fort St. John, with a policeman as passenger. About halfway there, the policeman asked, "Aren't you going to call?" meaning call ahead to the airport. Don said no, as he had not been shown how to operate the HF crystal radio, nor did he feel any urgency to use it. The policeman volunteered to show him, and since this seemed unlikely to cause any harm, Don agreed. They reeled out a wire aerial, and when the mike was keyed to transmit, Don got an electrical shock, confirming his lack of enthusiasm for the device. Nevertheless, the radio worked and Don acquired a new skill.

The Pilot's Wife—No Easy Life

Irene Carson graduated from the University of Alberta nursing school in the spring of 1939. She and Don were married July 30, 1940, at Edmonton's St. Alphonsus Church, headquarters for the Redemptorist Missionaries working throughout the north and one block from the house where Irene grew up. They had gone to high school together and had been dating for about as long as Don had been flying, so she had

Don and Irene Patry about to leave Edmonton on honeymoon, July 31, 1940.
D.V. Patry collection

some idea of what she was getting into. She was working as a teaching nurse in Edmonton, and Don was often away. "I didn't see very much of him around this time." Periodically, Don would get tired of the isolation and the constant complaining by Scotty Moir and Sheldon Luck, and pack up his kit and head for home, telling Grant McConachie that he'd had enough, he quit. Grant didn't want to lose a good pilot, so he'd do the only sensible thing he could, which was nothing. After a few days off, Don would return, and it was business as usual until the next time he needed a break. If Don had not occasionally rebelled, he never would have been home at all.

Their marriage was structured around flying. To Irene, it was matter of fact: "You adjusted your life for flying right from the start." The wedding was held on a Tuesday so they could start their honeymoon on Don's flight out on the next day. Scotty Moir was flying the Barkley Grow with Don in the right seat, and for a while it looked like Irene wasn't going to be in any seat at all. Barney Philips, the flight ops manager, said that due to a doctors' convention, the plane was full of paying passengers and Irene would have to wait. Fortunately, a gentleman on company business volunteered his seat so Irene could go on her honeymoon!

Once on the plane, Irene discovered, to her discomfort, that one of her fellow passengers was Dr. Huckle from the University Hospital. There was a very distinct hierarchy at the hospital during training, and the doctors tended to be very authoritarian toward the nursing staff. Irene respected Dr. Huckle, but felt uncomfortable sitting right beside him in the close confines of the small plane. Thankfully, Dr. Huckle did not recognize her. After some time, Irene realized that the bench seat with the rod and curtain where she and Dr. Huckle were sitting was actually the toilet. What an equalizer! She could hardly contain her laughter, thinking, "I'm sitting at the back of a Barkley Grow with Dr. Huckle on the toilet!"

The doctors got off the plane at Grande Prairie, the seats were removed, and the aircraft was loaded with freight. Irene ended up sitting on a coil of rope all the way to Fort St. John. The next stop was Charlie Lake; here Irene was cautioned to "watch out for Ma Powell." Evalyn, or "Ma" was the wife of Walter "Red" Powell. She was a pioneering mother of a large family, with a well-deserved reputation for pulling practical jokes on the unsuspecting. This time, however, Ma resisted the temptation to prank the newlyweds, and the next day they were off to Vancouver and a welcome honeymoon.

They returned to their "new" home at Fort St. John, a small log cabin rented from a local trapper, Joe Clark. When Don had asked how much the rent was, Joe replied, "Five dollars per month; is that too much?" They bought three hundred and fifty dollars worth of furniture on credit from a store in Edmonton, and had it shipped up by rail. Lighting was provided by a gas lamp that they had received as a wedding present. There was no well, but water was available for twenty-five cents a barrel. The washroom was an outhouse, which a local odd-job man named Harvey was hired to spruce up. When Irene asked Harvey for his bill, he presented her with a bill for eighteen and a half hours of labour for "whitewashing outhouse." The total owed was $2.50, a reasonable

Don and Irene Patry, Fort St. John, BC, 1940.
Flag at far left belongs to the Hudson Bay Store.
D.V. Patry collection

amount despite the exaggerated hours. They also bought a radio that could receive the frequency used by the planes, 5390 KC, so Irene would know when Don was back at base. There was no cookstove in the cabin, so the boys from the airport liberated a slightly beat-up one that had been left behind by the American work crew who had built the Fort St. John runway. Later, Joe replaced this stove with a new one. The cupboards were orange crates nailed to the wall.

Late for Supper

On October 1, 1940, Don was flying the Barkley Grow CF-BMW, loaded with freight, into Fort Nelson, and then heading southwest to Deadman Lake, now called Tuchodi Lake. Eighteen-year-old Bob Hammond, mechanic and aspiring engineer, was sitting in the right-hand seat, enjoying his second ever ride in an airplane and hoping to get some experience working the radio. Bob's first ride had been with Chief Pilot Ted Field, and ominously enough, they had been struck by lightning during the flight. Bob didn't know it at the time, but lightning was about to strike twice.

At Deadman Lake, they were scheduled to pick up a party of big-game hunters from Carlyle, Illinois, one of whom was a Dr. Wilson Ducomb, and then fly to Charlie Lake. While at Fort Nelson, it came to Don's attention that the station manager, Leo McKinnon, had a bad toothache. Don told him to come along on the flight so he could get to a dentist. Also boarding at Fort Nelson was "the old game warden from Prince George, Van Dyke was his name, and he'd been in the First World War, he'd been gassed, and shot, and his jaw was all out of shape. He was sort of a cranky old fella; anyway, he was at Fort Nelson and he wanted to get out."

Since they hadn't known just when they would be picked up, the hunting party did not start to break camp until BMW arrived. "They never knew when you were going to get in to pick them up; it could be a week late if the weather wasn't suitable." They had a lot of tents, equipment, and trophy sheep heads. By the time everything was packed and loaded, it was getting late, almost dusk. They departed Deadman Lake with clear conditions on top and some smoky haze below. Very shortly, however, there was a solid undercast ahead. Don wasn't too concerned at this point, as he had a couple of options. The first was to call Fort St. John and get an update from the radio operator, Tony Craig. The second was to tune in the low-frequency 272 kHz non-directional beacon in order to make use of an Automatic Direction Finder (ADF). "It wasn't a proper ADF; it didn't swing and point and give you a reading and a heading. It was just a left/right needle, and you picked it up and if the needle was over to the left, why, you centred it by going to the left until it was centred."

Yukon Southern Air Transport (YSAT) Barkley Grow CF-BMW "Yukon Prince",
chief pilot Ted Field standing on float, Charlie Lake, BC, 1941.
D.V. Patry collection

Repeat calls to Tony—"Charlie Lake BMW, Charlie Lake BMW"—
went unanswered. At first, Don wondered if the guys at the base were
goofing around, but it was soon obvious that they could not establish
voice contact. All they were able to receive was Morse code from Tony
on the carrier signal: dash dot, dash dash dot. These were the letters N
and G, indicating reception no good. However, it appeared that they
did have a signal for the direction needle. "The needle was off to the
left-hand side, if I remember right, and I was trying to catch up to it,
and first thing I knew, I did a 360 and the needle was still there. I had
two aerials, so I switched and flipped over to the other side. I did a 360
that way and it was still there. By this time, doing the 360s, I'd lost the
heading that I was on, so I just picked up a heading and I figured when
I got close to the lake, if I was close, they could hear me and I could
talk to them. But I never did get to talk to them, and we were running
out of gas."

Don flew on, estimating the correct heading, the clouds and smoke
below preventing him from sighting anything on the ground that might
give them a clue of their position. Bob Hammond was no longer just
along for the ride, but desperately staring down and searching for a
break in the clouds that might offer escape. One by one, the fuel tanks
ran dry: "That airplane had six tanks and they only have about fifteen
gallons each, and I kept running out of tanks; we used to run 'em dry,
and they were popping like mad." After switching to the last tank, Don
said what everyone had been thinking: "Bobby, we have to land."

Back at the cabin, Irene had the radio tuned to the 5390 frequency.
When she heard Don's first call to Tony, she started the fire in the
cookstove, expecting him to be home shortly and hungry at the end
of a long day. Until now, it had always been comforting to hear the
transmissions and know where Don was and that he was safe. This time,
the radio provided only anxiety as the emergency unfolded before her.
Irene could hear both Don and Tony, but frustratingly, they could not
hear each other. The tension increased with Don's last call: "Charlie
Lake, BMW, I see a hole; I'm going down."

Whatever happened next was going to be strictly between Don, his airplane, and Saint Christopher. There was no communications, navigation, or co-pilot help; he was on his own. "There was sort of a hole in the cloud and below it kinda looked like a lake, and so down we went. This airplane had flares, and I said to Bob, 'We'll fly over this and have a look and I'll pull a flare.' Just as we were coming up on it, well, I pulled the flare and *boom*, there was a big explosion and flash and it went out! But anyway, I was committed, and I continued the approach. I put the landing lights on and the fog and haze just threw a glare right back in my face, so I turned them off again and flicked 'em on at the very last, and, golly, the trees were there. So, that poor little airplane; I firewalled it, and I think you could have heard it clear down to Vancouver!

"It was fairly light, there was no gas in the airplane to speak of, so we climbed out of there nice and I went around on a 180 (a shallow 180-degree turn, followed by flying downwind for approximately one minute, followed by a second 180-degree turn) and came back. I thought, well, I'll pull a flare again, which I did, and the same thing happened." The next day, when the flares and attached parachutes were spotted hanging from trees, it became clear why the flares seemed to fizzle—the plane was so low that the flares had no time to burn before dropping into the treetops.

"So we went around again. This time I left the lights off until the edge of the trees quit and I knew there should be water in front of that, closed the throttle, and landed. It was a smooth landing, but boy, was it a little lake, a slough!" Somehow they had safely landed on an unnamed puddle of water, at night, in instrument conditions. Later, Don found out that had he flown for another ten minutes, they would have been in the mountains.

Don taxied in until the inside float was in the muck and the wing close to shore. There was still no radio contact with Tony, so the plan was to pull out an aerial that was on a reel and see if that would work. Bob got out on the wing with the aerial and jumped onto the bank, slipping off and sinking up to his knees in the muck. Eventually, he extricated himself and hung the wire from a tree. Leo was next out and just as graceful. "Leo, he forgot all about his toothache after two tries at landing, and he gets out on the wing and he'd seen what happened to Bobby, so he made a big jump. The ground was froze; it was sorta late in the fall, and he landed spread-eagle and pretty near killed himself.

"The doctor, he was a pretty decent fellow. He was a little perturbed about not getting home; I don't know if he had to be home at a certain time or not, but it didn't matter—we were stuck there for the night. Old Van Dyke, he wouldn't get out of the airplane and he didn't get out until morning. Leo was a comical guy, a real entertainer, and he kept everybody laughing. We built a fire, had some rations, and finally went to sleep."

Tony sent Kay Osborne and a friend over to Irene with the message that, although he still had no communication with Don, he could tell from the carrier signal that Don had attempted to call after the plane went down. This suggested that they had landed safely. Tony also wanted her to know that he would monitor the radio during the night, which he did, staying on duty right through until the next day.

The next morning, Don was able to communicate with Scotty Moir, who was flying another YSAT Barkley Grow, CF-BMG, from Edmonton. Don briefed him on their situation and described the location as best he could. Scotty relayed this information to a trapper who knew the area, and he was able to figure out approximately where Don was relative to Charlie Lake. Scotty made a quick stop at Grande Prairie and then Fort St. John. There he teamed up with YSAT employees Stan Emery and Glen Fenby, loaded three ten-gallon drums of gas, and went looking for BMW. After unsuccessfully following Don's directions, Scotty managed to find the slough and was quick to tell Don what he thought of his sense of direction. As BMG was equipped with wheeled landing gear, it was impossible for Scotty to land. His only option was to try an airdrop, which was something new for all involved. Concentrating at the controls, he flew over low and fast, while in the rear of the plane, Stan and Glen braced themselves and got ready to drop the drums.

Extra speed is good for flying, but not so good for dropping cargo. "When he pushed a barrel, it came tumbling out of the airplane and it hit the water and just flattened. There was just a blue haze; that's all you could see, and the barrel looked like a pie plate. All three the same thing." Thirty gallons of gas gone, and plane and passengers still stranded on the ground.

It was time to improvise. Don drained the gas from the auxiliary tanks of BMW into a waxed cardboard cylinder airsickness container, and then poured it into one main tank. Don estimated that it would be enough to get to Charlie Lake if the load was lightened. "So we cleaned the airplane out; we even got old Van Dyke out and all of the game hunters' trophies."

Don asked Bob if he wanted to fly out with him, and Bob did a quick mental review: on his first flight, he was struck by lightning; on the second flight, he had a front-row seat for a black-hole landing at night; the third would be in a plane running on fumes. Not surprisingly, he replied, "Thanks, Smoke, but I think I'll just wait here."

The wind was blowing from the wrong direction for an immediate takeoff, so Don taxied downwind, turned, and with minimum delay had the empty plane airborne on Scotty's heading back to Charlie Lake. "I took off and stayed on top of the trees, throttled back and picked up my heading, and went straight in and landed. Before I could get to the dock, I was out of gas, the red warning lights were popping, the engines were about to quit. I pulled up to the dock, put some gas in the airplane, and went back and picked everybody up and brought 'em back, landed, and damned if the company didn't send me on to Whitehorse!"

After getting word that everybody was okay, that afternoon, Irene attended a tea party, one of the town's few social events. She expected Don to be home when she got back, but to her surprise he was gone again. It wasn't until the next evening that they finally had supper together, two days late.

As a footnote to the story, Dr. Ducomb was interviewed by a reporter and spoke enthusiastically about the adventure. "It was the neatest bit of piloting I have ever seen. I have been on six big-game hunting trips, but this was the most exciting of all."

Flights on the Lighter Side

In December 1940, Irene moved back to Edmonton and rented a small apartment and furniture for the winter. Red Powell's truck, carrying her and a few possessions, was the first to cross the ice bridge on the Peace River that winter. The furniture and cabin at Fort St. John were rented to a policeman. A contributing factor to the move south was Irene's pregnancy, and the following April she gave birth to a baby boy named Ken, who would follow in his father's footsteps and grow up to be a pilot with Air Canada. After the move to Edmonton, Irene saw very little of Don, who was still flying out of Fort St. John. He was kept busy flying, and if it wasn't for his own scheming, he probably wouldn't have gotten home at all.

A typical example involved one of the company planes, a Beech Staggerwing. Ted Field, Chief Pilot based out of Edmonton, had mentioned that the Staggerwing's engine would need to be rebuilt before long. Don and another budding engineer, Glen Fenby, decided that this could be a ticket to Edmonton and some time off. On a day that Grant and Barney were flying to Vancouver in the Barkley, Glen and Don rose early and slipped away in the Staggerwing. The weather was poor and they had to stay glued to the railroad track to find their way. Ted was surprised to see them arrive in Edmonton, and asked why they were there. "Well," Don replied, "you said the engine needed to be rebuilt." Always frugal, Ted replied, "It had two or three hours left and you just used it up!" Regardless, the boys got their time off.

Grant and Barney had an interesting flight that day as well. Grant had asked the metal bashers at maintenance to build a couple of engine heaters from small coal oil stoves. These could be left on overnight so the engines were preheated by morning. A fellow by the name of Bill Given was in charge of heating the Barkley Grow, and seeing as how the stoves would be on all night, he turned the burners down low. What he didn't realize was that this caused them to smoke, and this sooty smoke drifted into the ductwork of the plane via a heater pipe from the stove to the cold-air inlet located in the front of the wing, close to the fuselage. No one noticed when the plane departed the next morning.

Once airborne, the cabin heat was turned on, and unbeknownst to Grant or Barney, a very fine carbon soot was drifting throughout the cockpit and sticking to their faces. When they arrived at Prince George in poor visibility, they had to stick their heads out the side windows to see the runway. This caused their eyes to water and tears to run, streaking their darkened faces. It wasn't until they were in the hotel room in Vancouver that they suddenly realized why they had been getting the funny looks from people along the way. Staring at each other's soot-streaked faces, they burst into laughter, unable to stop until the tears rolled once again.

Surprise Visit to Deace Lake—Emergency Landing on an Ice Cube
Range stations used for radio navigation aids were located at Fort Nelson, Watson Lake, Whitehorse, and Fort St. John. Sometime around December 1941, a fire in the Watson Lake powerhouse destroyed the generator used to power the range station, and a replacement engine was needed. There was some urgency involved, since the American air force was ferrying aircraft through Canada up to Alaska and relied on the range stations to navigate the unfamiliar territory. From Alaska, Russian pilots flew the planes on to Russia.

An engine was available at Prince George, and on December 15, 1941, Don and Harvey Johnston were assigned to transport it to Watson Lake in a Lockheed 14 that had the passenger seats removed. Also on board was a DOT man who was responsible for the installation of the replacement engine. At Prince George, the engine and parts were loaded and the plane departed into an overcast sky.

Over the radio, Watson Lake was reporting clear weather conditions, but the 14 was in cloud and starting to pick up ice. Don pulled the plane up on top of the cloud and the icing stopped. However, before long they were back in cloud with a buildup of ice, and Don could not coax the 14 to climb any higher. After a brief descent, they found themselves between cloud layers, but it was raining and the icing continued. Generally, these conditions require a climb or a descent to find an ice-free altitude. In this case, climbing was out of the question since it was all Don could do to maintain altitude, and he was reluctant to drop down because he didn't know where the mountains were.

Suddenly, they spotted a hole in the clouds, and immediately dropped a wing and spiralled down through the opening to level out in a valley with a river below. They decided to follow the river downstream, trusting it would lead them to something recognizable. Just as they were about to head up another valley, they saw a small lake. "Harv said, 'Let's go over there and see how big a lake it is.' We went around the corner and this lake just opened up in front of us, and I said, 'It's Deace Lake!' There was a Hudson's Bay store on one side of the lake, and Harv knew the people that ran it. We could see this little patch of ice along the shore, a runway. It wasn't very long, I'd say about twelve hundred feet. They had it marked off for Russ Baker, who was going to ferry gas into Watson Lake. He had a Junkers on skis and was waiting for the lake to freeze enough to hold the airplane. I forget how many inches there was, but five inches would have held an airplane real good, especially on skis.

"We tried every valley out of there to get to Watson Lake. We were talking to the Watson Lake people on the radio and apparently they did have a low-powered engine sort of running the range station, but we couldn't pick it up. We couldn't get out of Deace Lake. The minute we pulled up into the clag, we iced up. So we tried to get down at the top end of Deace. The Deace River runs right out of the lake into the Liard River, and if we could have followed that river, why, we would have made it, because Lower Post is on the Liard River just about six or seven miles from Watson Lake. But it was all just plugged right in, and we'd try another valley. We tried two or three valleys out of there. Finally, we were running low of gas, so we had to do something, land or try and pull up. Well, we couldn't pull up because we would ice up. We were talking to Whitehorse and they said that the ice runway had a couple or three inches of ice on it. Not enough to hold a Lockheed with a ton of engine in pieces in the back.

"So, after thinking it over, well, we couldn't do anything else, so we're gonna have to land. We went around and got down and as soon as we touched down, I just kept it going right up to the dock, thinking the minute we closed the throttle or stopped, it was gonna sink! But it didn't, we heaved a sigh of relief, and we were on terra firma. Harv knew the Hudson's Bay man and we were welcomed there. I remember that night we slept in the upstairs part above the store, and it had a tin roof and the weather sort of warmed up a wee bit and this ice slid off the tin roof with a clatter you wouldn't believe; we thought we'd had it! The next morning, it was nice clear weather, the plane hadn't sunk, and we had enough gas to make Watson Lake, so we took off and wound up at Watson Lake.

"About two weeks later, a Pan American DC-3 with a captain by the name of Knox got into the same predicament; they couldn't get through flying VFR. They knew about this place and that we had landed there, so they went back and landed. During the night, I guess there was a chinook come up, and when they got up in the morning, the water was right up practically to the top of the wheels. I guess they got a little excited and they tried to hurry things up to get out of there, and they got an engine on fire. So they were stuck. We had a pilot in Whitehorse named Bob Goldie; he was flying a Pilgrim. It was a big ten-passenger single-engine airplane that United Airlines used for their cross-country work. Bob was flying it on skis. He picked up a couple of Pan Am engineers and their tools, and flew them down to Deace Lake. Then Bob took the Pan Am passengers over to Watson Lake. The engineers got the DC-3 started, and they were able to take off and come to Watson."

The Stew That Left 'em Breathless

"One time, Stan Emery and I were flying on a passenger scheduled run from Fort St. John to Prince George to Vancouver. Melba Tamney was the stewardess. It was overcast with icing conditions, and out of Prince George we always climbed as high as possible to get well clear of the mountains. We got up to about seventeen thousand feet and of course had the oxygen masks on, and got over the Vancouver outer marker, the Maple Ridge Fan Marker on the east leg of the range, where we could go down to nine thousand feet. This was the first time I had gone into Vancouver on instruments in the 14, and Stan had very little instrument experience, period. So we were busy. I guess we flew on blind trust. When you had a twin engine airplane, you figured it could do anything."

To say this was a stressful situation would be a major understatement. Don and Stan were scanning the instruments like their lives depended on it, which was true. At this moment, Melba attempted to come into the cockpit to inform the captain that she had shut off the oxygen supply, as they were low enough that it wasn't needed. However, she didn't get a chance to say a word, as Don was so focused on the task at hand that he was a little abrupt. Melba was not the kind of person who would stand for that, regardless of the circumstances.

"I told Melba, 'Not now, go away,' and waved her off. Well, she slammed that door almost off the hinges on the way out. Stan and I kept sucking away on the oxygen down to six thousand feet. The green bags on the masks were popped out, ready to burst, because we weren't getting any air! We got in okay and it wasn't until later that we found out what had happened. No grudges, though; we all laughed about it!"

The Fifty-Hour Wonder

"This was a bad one for me; I think it was about 1942. I was flying a 14 down to Vancouver. I had this first officer, he was a brand new guy, the poor fella he didn't have much time at all, what we called a fifty-hour wonder. He had a commercial licence, of course, but he was pretty green.

"The 14s with the 850-horsepower Wrights, they only had one generator. We were headed across from Fort St. John to Prince George at night, and the first thing I noticed was that the panel lights were dimming. Going dimmer, dimmer, and then the airspeed started slowing up and acting erratic, and then it quit. I then noticed with a flashlight that I had a load of ice on and my pitot had iced up and I'd lost my airspeed. We did have an emergency radio—this airplane had come from TCA [Trans Canada Airlines], so it was a little better equipped than some others on the line. It was a nice plane, built for a pilot. We could talk to the tower and we could read the range, so I thought we'd be okay.

"So going into Prince George, it was snowing, and visibility was pretty low. I got on the south leg and let down, and when I went to put the landing light on, it came out halfway and that was it, no landing light. When I saw the runway, we were too far down. We couldn't land; we'd have been off the end. I asked this poor guy—I won't mention any names, as he actually wound up to be a senior pilot with CPA—to lift the gear and then the flaps. Very, very slowly, lift the flaps up. Well, he just dumped 'em!"

This was a major error at a very critical time. Raising the gear would streamline the plane and allow the airspeed to increase. Lifting the flaps would do the same thing but also cause a loss in lift, so it has to be done in stages to ensure that airspeed increases to compensate for the reduced lift. Otherwise, the plane could suddenly descend.

Luckily, steady nerves, faith, and Don's previous experience with seat-of-the-pants flying gave them a fighting chance. "And this poor airplane, I had no airspeed, trying to climb out of there in the cloud at night with ice on. That airplane has ninety-degree flaps, and when they come down, boy, it slows you up. I poured the coal to it and just sort of read what I had, altimeter. The windshield was iced up, but there was a little window that we could pull up, about a quarter of the windshield on a slant, you could open that up and sort of hang out and see. I did a 180 and back around, I followed that leg about three or four minutes anyway to make sure I was far enough away. We came back around over the range station and got in that time, but oh boy, I don't know how we managed to stay in the air, climbing out of that approach."

There was no post-flight follow-up or discussion about this incident. "Not a thing. CPA didn't ask questions like that, and it wasn't until about 1943 that they got some bigger shots in the company that had come from TCA. They'd want to know all about things; you had to write a report and all that. Before that, things were pretty lax. Family members didn't even need passes to get on the airplane; they just got on.

"The first time we ran into pass problems was when I took Irene up to Whitehorse. Passes had come in by then, but I didn't know that (and didn't care). The next morning, this company guy was checking and was really sneaky—somehow he got wind that Irene was on the airplane without this special pass and he was gonna blow the whistle. Anyway, between the stewardess and the first officer, they hoodwinked him and wouldn't let him know Irene was on the airplane. He was trying his darndest to find out, but Jack Barber, the traffic man at Whitehorse, was in on it too, and the inspector got nowhere.

"When I eventually got to Edmonton, I went in to see Grant and I said, 'I guess I did a no-no?' All he said was, 'Oh, I already know,' and that's all there was to it, but from then on we had to make arrangements ahead of time."

Lodestars from Texas, or Getting Out of Dallas by Sunrise

In May of 1942, Don and Irene bought a house in Edmonton for the sum of thirty-two hundred dollars, with five hundred dollars down. They had hardly settled into the new house when word came from the coast that most of the pilots were out of action with whooping cough, and Don was needed to go out and fly the route out of Vancouver. So in July, they packed up and moved into the Devonshire Hotel in downtown Vancouver, a comfortable place with a small kitchenette. As would be expected, Don got a cough, although he was able to keep flying. Eventually, the other pilots recovered, and in late June, Don,

Irene, and fourteen-month-old Ken moved back to the house in Edmonton. Very shortly thereafter, Don was on the move again: Grant McConachie wanted Don to accompany him on a trip to Texas to bring back a couple of Lockheed Lodestars. It would be a short routine trip. The trouble was, with Grant, nothing was ever routine.

The Canadian Pacific Railway had formed Canadian Pacific Air Lines (CPA) in 1942 by buying and amalgamating Canadian Airways, McKenzie Air Services, and Yukon Southern Air Transport. Grant McConachie was the western manager for CPA. It was a somewhat chaotic and exciting time, with a lot of American military activity related to the Alaska Highway and the Alaska–Siberia Lend Lease program. This meant increased demand for CPA to transport people and cargo, and increased demand for more planes, which were scarce. Somehow, with some political horse trading and backroom deals between CPA and the US and Canadian governments, Grant had lined up two planes in Texas. So now he needed to go and get them.

"From Edmonton, we went out to Vancouver and got our passports and all that sort of stuff. We went with United Airlines to Seattle in a DC-3 and talked to Carl Squier, the boss man at the Lockheed plant where the planes had been built. These planes were now in Dallas, Texas, in a holding pen, so we had to go there. I don't know who owned them, if it was Lockheed or the US government." One theory is that these planes were destined for the Dutch East Indies, but transfer was pre-empted by the Japanese invasion of that country on January 11, 1942. If the Dutch government had paid for the planes, they would be the owners. In any event, the USAF was likely happy to be rid of them.

"Anyway, it was quite a hassle. We flew commercial to LA, then across the mountains at night. I remember trying to sleep and we wound up in Dallas. Then the Lockheed people came down to Texas and the battle was trying to get these things paid for, or get title to them. McConachie was on the phone to Larry Unwin, the vice-prezy of CPR, and it battled back and forth, and there were telegrams and Lord knows what all. Finally, I don't think we were ever really clear; Grant got the

Canadian Pacific Airlines Lockheed Lodestar CF-CPA over the Rocky Mountains, circa 1943. One of the planes Don and Grant McConachie "stole".
Nicholas Morant

head honchos sort of on a party one night and it was all settled. Grant was in cahoots with the boss man at Lockheed, who wanted him to get the planes because of CPR influence. We got the planes, but I think we actually stole them.

"I didn't see what they agreed to, but Grant said everything was taken care of, and the next day we're out early to the airport, before it got daylight, really, and the aircraft were all gassed up and ready to go. They had a first officer for me, a young fellow from Texas; apparently, you had to have one. I don't know why; the plane only had one set of instruments. Grant had Hans Broten, the radio operator from Edmonton; he must have come down when they got close to an agreement. Anyway, we flew back as far as Butte, Montana. I was thirsty and went into the terminal building and got a pop, and coming back out, there was a man standing there with a uniform on. He wanted to know where I came from and how I got in there. I said, 'Well, I come

CPA Lockheed Lodestar CF-CPB, c/n 2179. One of the
planes Don and Grant McConachie "stole".
CP Railways

in this gate and I'm going out this gate to get in that airplane!' I had a
heck of a time to prove I was the pilot.

"Bill Straight flew down to Butte with someone in the little Stinson.
He was superintendent of flight operations. Hans got in with me to
relieve the American. We landed in Edmonton in the afternoon, and I
just got out of the airplane and went home. The next morning, they
put those airplanes, CF-CPA and CF-CPB, right to work, camouflage paint
and all.

"Herbert Hollick-Kenyon was the superintendent of that part of
the airline. The Lodestars were used for everything, hauling people and
equipment. Sitting on those bench seats, looking at the other passengers,
it was easy to get airsick. Lunches were bagged. Eventually, they got
proper seats and took the camouflage paint off."

"We had a couple of Boeing 247-DS and two of the 14s, and then
Grant made the deal getting the Lodestars, which had 1,200-horsepower

engines. They were building the pipeline from Fort McMurray to Whitehorse at that time; the project was run by a company named Bechel, Price and Callaghan. They were just crying for airplanes; they'd fly anything they could get their hands on. The aircraft people were just building fighters for the war, so other planes were in short supply.

"Ted Field and I checked out a flying boat in Vancouver that hadn't been flown for half a dozen years, anyway. It belonged to the forestry people in Vancouver. It was a Boeing, about the second Boeing that they ever built in Seattle. Canadian Airways had flown this thing, used it in the fisheries up and down the coast. It was put away in the back of a hangar, and by golly, they dug it out, worked on the engine, fired it up, and Ted and I flew it.

"It was a funny thing to fly. Before you could get enough speed to get the nose out of the water, why, the water just come all over the windshield and you thought you were going to drown. Then it would pop out of the water and it was a real good performer. Bob Goldie flew that thing up on the pipeline. There was another twin-engine plane—they called it 'Nip and Tuck;' I forget the actual name of it—but Harvey Johnston flew it from Edmonton up to Whitehorse and it went on the pipeline too."

After the trip to Texas, things got settled down and Don was home more. He had been promoted to Chief Pilot, replacing Sheldon Luck, who had joined Ferry Command headquartered in Montreal. Don was even home for Christmas in 1942, for the first time since he had started flying.

The Characters

Walter and Evalyn Powell ran the Imperial Oil dealership at Charlie Lake, Fort St. John, BC. They had a business arrangement with Grant McConachie to provide fuel, accommodation, and meals for YSAT. Grant benefited greatly from their willingness to extend credit and act as a buffer when Imperial management became concerned with overdue accounts, which was often. They also operated a farm and a sawmill, and did some trucking. With nine children, they did whatever it took to get by. Everyone called them Red and Ma, and they were well-known in the area.

"The Powells at Charlie Lake were a real colourful family, Ma and Red. They had a bunch of kids; those boys that became pilots had some real good stories to tell. They established quite a reputation from their adventures. They were big-game hunters, and one time one of them got clobbered by a grizzly bear, but somehow he managed to escape.

"They were also great practical jokers. Newlyweds Rose and Leo McKinnon really got it when they stayed there; they were inclined to drench you with a bucket of water as you went into your bedroom, or ketchup, or rig your bed so it would collapse. Just about anything they could think of, and they had some help from the maintenance boys in the bunkhouse too, you know. They were all practical jokers, and they had time on their hands between the flights to think up new shenanigans.

"One time McConachie was up there with some bigwig, and we were in the bunkhouse attached to the Powell house. The mechanics were in their own bunkhouse. Ernie Kubicek was in one bunk, I was in another, and Alec Dane was there too. All of a sudden, what looked like a bomb came in through the window! It was a piece of radiator hose made to look like a stick of dynamite, and it had a fuse that was burning away. There was no powder, of course, but we didn't know that.

"Well, holy smoke! Alec jumped out of his bunk, but couldn't get out of his sleeping bag. Grant got out of his and he went right up to the mechanics' hut; he was really mad that this foolery was going on in front of his guest, and he fired Bill Gibbons right on the spot. But of course before long he hired him back, and Bill wound up getting his engineer's ticket and becoming a supervisor for CPA in Vancouver."

One-Eyed Tommy
"Stan Emery and I left Fort Nelson and flew over to the rapids in the Liard River called Hell's Gate. The land there really shrunk right into

a narrow, narrow valley. It was in the fall, and when we got into this valley, the visibility just went blotto. It was a bad place to be flying if you couldn't see, so I pulled the plane up in a real tight turn, around and back out again.

"We went back to Fort Nelson and this old trader there, Tommy Clark, he was a rum man, and he always had a case of rum. Since we couldn't fly anyway, Stan and I got into the rum and we sure tied one on. There was an old club bag there and somehow somebody fell into it, I'm not gonna say who, and it closed like a bear trap around his neck. We still laugh about that. The next day, the visibility was good but our heads were foggy; we shouldn't have been flying 'cause we were both hurting.

"Tommy was well-known for a variety of reasons, but especially for his glass eye. He had a trading post at Fort Nelson and he had the Indians under his control. He was part Indian himself: his father was a Scotsman, a trader. He'd take that glass eye out and put it in the crook of a tree and say to the Indians, 'My eye can see you! Make sure you bring all the furs you get back to me. I can see you!' I flew him around a lot for bartering and fur buying, and he was quite a character."

CHAPTER FOUR: **HELPING THE US MILITARY**

Million Dollar Valley

On Sunday, December 7, 1941, at 8 AM, Pearl Harbor, on the Island of Oahu, Hawaii, was attacked by the Japanese Imperial Navy. There had been no declaration of war; the attack was a surprise, and the Americans were caught napping. This signalled the entry of the US into World War Two and resulted in considerable American military activity in Canada, both in the air and on the ground, since Canada was a critical link between mainland USA and Alaska.

From 1942 through 1945, under the Alaska–Siberia Lend Lease program, American crews delivered almost eight thousand aircraft through Canada to Soviet aircrews for their war effort. US pilots flew the planes from Great Falls, Montana, to airfields in Alberta, British Columbia, and the Yukon, and on to Fairbanks, following the Northwest Staging Route pioneered by Grant McConachie. The planes were transferred to the Russians at Ladd Field in Fairbanks and then flown to Siberia via Galena and Nome, where they were eventually used in the Soviet war effort against Germany.

A few of the planes never made it to Ladd Field. On January 16, 1942, five B-26 Marauders crash-landed, three in the same location. This famous crash created the legend of the Million Dollar Valley, the valley of the crashed planes, and caused Don to receive personal correspondence from a Brigadier General of the US Army.

At around 11 AM, ten B-26s from the 77th Bombardment Squadron had taken off from Edmonton, headed for Whitehorse in the Yukon. They broke off into smaller groups and one flight of three became lost between Fort Nelson and Watson Lake. Given the circumstances, it would have been surprising if they hadn't gotten lost: low-time pilots with no bush-flying experience, pencil sketch maps, a thousand miles to fly, waning daylight, problems with the radio range, and a bit of snow thrown in for good measure. Running low on fuel, they found a fairly level area to land in a large, shallow, snow-covered valley near the Upper Grayling River, one hundred and eleven miles southeast of Watson Lake.

"The first guy went in, dumped the gear, dirtied it up with flaps and everything down, and of course he busted up. The two others take the gear up and went in nice and smooth, like a big toboggan in the deep snow. They could have landed on the lake [Toobally Lake] about fifteen miles north of them. They could see it, but they had been told don't land on the ice 'cause it won't hold. It was lots thick enough, but they didn't know that."

In 1990 Howard Smiley, the co-pilot of Marauder 40-1464 , wrote an account of this crash. He recalled that pilot William J. Dancer Jr. was ejected throught the windshield while he remained in the plane but was knocked unconscious. Luckily their injuries were minor and the rest of the crew were fine. On January 18, around noon, the downed planes were spotted by a flight of P-40Es from the Eleventh Pursuit Squadron headed for Watson Lake. The crews were flown out the next day without incident.

US B-26 Marauder 401464 crash landing enroute to Russia, "Million Dollar Valley," January 16, 1942. The million dollar reference was an estimate of the value of the planes wrecked that day.
Howard Smiley collection

The other part of the story concerns the two other Marauders that also met their fate that day, at two different airports. As Don explains, "Two Marauders made it to Watson Lake, and by the time they got there it was almost dark. We used to put spruce boughs out on the lake; the runway crossed a sort of peninsula, and we spread boughs to lead you in. You came in over the lake and followed them in, but the runway started right at the bank. The first guy came in and he landed okay. The guy that was following, he got down a bit too low and run right into the bank and bounced up in the air and landed on his nose on the airport.

"Harvey Johnston and I had come in from Vancouver with a Lockheed 14 up to Whitehorse. There was a load of freight to go to Dawson City, so Harv and I took this load. We left early in the morning [January 16], and there were four or five Marauders sitting in Whitehorse that had got there before. They ploughed the snow when we left, and there was a little ridge left on the side of the runway. When we left, these guys were getting their engines warmed up and ready to take off for Fairbanks. When we came back, there was an aircraft scattered all over the runway. What had happened was, he started his takeoff, and the Marauders had electric props, and one prop ran away. The crankshaft broke or something, and the good engine pulled the aircraft over and this really high-rpm prop hit this snowbank and it just exploded. A blade went in through the side of the fuselage and the first officer, I understand it, broke his arm and the blade went up the side of his ribs and broke his collarbone. The injured were in the army hospital when we got back.

"It was a nice warm day; the snow was melting, and we had the windows open in the second-floor room we had in the old hotel. We had just got cleaned up and were going down to have a moose steak when we heard somebody hollering about where was the crew that had been flying the 14. Jack Barber was the station manager at Whitehorse. He found us and said they wanted us to go to Watson Lake and pick up the crew that crashed; one of them was badly hurt.

"On the flight up from Vancouver, we had a stewardess who was a nurse, Melba Tamney. So Melba and her boyfriend, Bob Goldie, who was flying out of Whitehorse at the time, came with us. Harv and I flew the airplane over to Watson Lake. When we got there, it was snowing a little bit, but the range was working and we had no problem landing. When we picked up the injured guys, the other crew was there, the ones that had landed first; they were all fine. I asked one of them why he didn't fly them to Whitehorse; he'd have been there six hours ago. He said, 'Man I wouldn't fly across those mountains at night for all the tea in China!' He was a young fella from Texas, never seen snow before.

"We flew the boys back to Whitehorse and turned them over to the army medical people, and I never heard anymore about it. I don't know how they made out except for reading some of the stories of that particular episode, and some of the things I read, doggone it, are not the way I heard it!"

While Don considered the rescue flight routine, the Headquarters Second Air Force, Fort George Wright, Washington, clearly did not. In early February 1942, Don received a letter that read in part: "I wish to take this opportunity of expressing to you and, through you, to your crew the appreciation of the personnel of the Second Air Force for the service rendered to fellow airmen, which not only served to mitigate their suffering but, perhaps, saved their lives." The letter was signed by John B. Brooks, Brigadier General, us Army, Commanding.

In 1971 an airplane restorer from California salvaged what remained of the Marauders, and 40-1464 was rebuilt. In 1992 it became the oldest B-26 still flying. An article on the salvage operation was published in the Spring 1976 issue of *Air Classics Quarterly*. The plane is now owned by collector Kermit Weeks of Florida.

Saving Alaska

Vancouver Province headline in 1943: "Two CPA Pilots Helped Save Alaska." The article went on to read, "Two commercial pilots, both well-known to Vancouver, made spine-tingling trips to Alaska with RCAF ground crew reinforcements when the Japanese unloaded bombs on Pearl Harbour, it was revealed today.

"They were Captain Don Patry, now senior Canadian Pacific Airlines pilot at Vancouver, and the late Captain Ernie W. Kubicek, who was pilot of the ill-starred CPA plane which crashed into Mount Cheam on December 21, 1942, killing its thirteen occupants.

"Grant McConachie, general manager of the CPA western lines, and Walter Gilbert, superintendent of the Mackenzie District of the CPA, told the story of CPA's role in the urgent work at Edmonton today in a Canadian Press report.

"The pilots and machines went on a war basis at the urgent request of Western Air Command of the RCAF, they said. Two loads of passengers, some enroute to Edmonton from Whitehorse, YT, and others northbound from Vancouver to the Yukon were 'jettisoned' at airfields along the route on notice of fifteen minutes. Both machines roared back to Vancouver and RCAF mechanics were taken aboard. The planes then winged for their destination at Anchorage in Alaska."

"'Every patrol bomber at Patricia Bay and at other bases along the southern coasts of British Columbia was rushed north,' Mr.Gilbert said. 'The payloads of these bombers, fully equipped for action, were so low that ground crews could not be carried. So that was where the CPA came in.'

"Air Vice-Marshal L.S. Stevenson, commanding officer of Western Air Command, made the request for planes to Mr. Gilbert through the Wing Commander Greenaway, then commanding the Patricia Bay operational station. The request was forwarded immediately to McConachie at Edmonton, who made the planes available."

Don's description was, as usual, somewhat low-key; Grant McConachie was always looking for opportunities to promote CPA, and he didn't hesitate to embellish a story if it would generate free publicity. Don, on the other hand, just told it as he saw it.

"I know I was headed for Vancouver and got the message around Prince George. Ernie Kubicek was headed north, and they stopped him at Prince George. He dumped his passengers and went back to Vancouver; nobody knew where we were going or what it was all about.

They were sending a squadron of airport people up to Alaska, because the Japs were trying to move into the Aleutian Islands. There was an RCAF group up there already and they were flying P-40's, but they needed bombers, these Blenheims. The pilots took the aircraft up, but they needed mechanics.

"We had 14s at that time, ten passengers, so we had ten mechanics each—they were all maintenance boys. We left Vancouver and went direct to Fort St. John, landed there and gassed up, and they said carry on to Whitehorse. So we went on to Whitehorse, gassed up, and they said you go on to Fairbanks. So we got to Fairbanks and wondered, now where do we go?

"We didn't know if we were going to China or the Aleutian Islands or what. At Fairbanks they said okay, you go down to Anchorage. Now I had never been to Anchorage, and neither had Ernie. There was a procedure; there was a little island that was to be used as a landmark. The airport at Anchorage was sort of the mainland but it jutted out. We were to fly over the island and make a right-hand turn and go around and line up with the runway. Ernie was ahead of me and he's coming up and it looked like he was going to go the other way!

"David Angus was my first officer, and I said to David, 'Holy smokes, Ernie's going the wrong way,' and all of a sudden he turned the right way, oh boy. There were machine guns down on this little island; you could see them following the airplane around. If he'd gone the wrong way, boom, he'd be blasted out of the air. But he made the right turn and we got on the ground there, and they said, 'Well, you're home. You're at the end of your trip?' So we just turned around and headed back to Fairbanks."

CHAPTER FIVE: **THE SEARCH FOR CPD**

Eleven Minutes From Safety

On December 20, 1942, CF-CPD, a Canadian Pacific Airways Lockheed Lodestar 14 with ten passengers and three crew members, disappeared without a trace on a flight from Fort St. John to Vancouver. The captain was thirty-four-year-old Ernie Kubicek, and the first officer was Bill Holland, aged thirty-eight. As with previous times of crisis for CPA, Don was again called upon, this time to help solve the mystery of a missing crew and passengers. "So they sent me out to Vancouver to look for Ernie."

In January Don and family once again moved out of their new home and headed west. Although Don's primary responsibility was to search for the missing plane, he would also be flying some of the scheduled runs.

Bill Holland had started his flying career as a bush pilot, and he later flew in the air force. After leaving the military, he went to fly for McConachie at CPA. He had the experience and qualifications to fly as captain, but before he jumped into the left seat, he was required to take a few flights as first officer to get familiarized with the company procedures and practices. Bill was a competent pilot who was willing to take calculated risks in order to get the job done. When he flew for Canadian Airways out of Vancouver, he was known to take off and climb into the clouds, heading across the island to Ucluelet and over the mountains just by timing himself, trusting that the winds and altimeter would not double-cross him when he had to let down.

Ernie was also a veteran pilot who had worked his way up from bush flying, and he had an old habit or two himself. If he saw an opening in the clouds when he was flying on instruments, he liked to get down and take a look to confirm where he was—he preferred to fly VFR just like he used to in the bush and rely on his own eyes, instead of some needles and dials. Nor was he afraid to push the weather, and on at least one occasion, this resulted in a landing that was nothing short of a miracle.

While steamboating along in a Norseman from Watson Lake to Whitehorse, Ernie had encountered a snowstorm, and decided to out climb it and find clear air. Before long he was flying blind in the thick of the mountains. He was living right that day, because somehow he flew onto the steep, snow-covered slope of a mountain so smoothly that his airspeed indicator slowly dropped to zero, even though he thought he was still flying! When he sorted out his situation, he was astonished to discover that there was not much damage to himself or the plane. When the weather cleared, he was able to report his position and was rescued. Incredibly, a few weeks later, after some repairs, he flew it off the mountain. That slope became known as Kubicek's Perch.

"Gord Ballentine, he was an old Canadian Airways pilot and writer. He flew the west coast most of his life; he's still writing stories. He was a good pilot, but boy, he was cautious. Gordie was at Fort St. John and had been hung up by weather for I don't know how many days. Ernie and Bill, they'd come from Vancouver up to Prince George, up to Fort St. John, and then they were on their way back, and Gord's still sitting at Fort St. John, waiting for the weather. Anyway, they met at Prince George and I guess Ernie said to Gordie, 'You finally got out of Fort St. John. Well, I'll beat you to Vancouver!'"

No one knows for sure what happened on that flight, but based on his own experience, Don had an educated guess. "I think what happened is they went over the mountains going from Prince George to Vancouver, and instead of following the range station down to Penticton and across to Princeton and then across into Vancouver, where they've got two range stations, Ernie heads direct to Vancouver. You used to intersect the east leg of the Vancouver range at Hope, and if you had an ADF in the airplane, you could home in on Seattle and it would take you right over the lake at Hope, but they didn't have an ADF in the thing, so you had to go by the range.

Memorial cairn for CF-CPD crash victims at Mount William Knight,
Cheam Range, BC. Plane disappeared on December 20, 1942 and
was discovered by Don Patry on August 9, 1943.
D.V. Patry collection

"This is my idea: he crossed the mountains and it didn't matter how much cloud there was; there would always be a break, especially if there was a wind. Ernie breaks out over Harrison and figures he's over Howe Sound, and boy, she's home. Except actually, they were over Harrison Lake at Chilliwack. It looks like Howe Sound—they're parallel, only Howe Sound is on the west side, in between the island and the mainland. They figured when they came out the end, Vancouver would be there. Well, it's getting dark and when they come out, there's no Vancouver lights. There are lights, but it would be Chilliwack, and at that point they're down below the cloud. They don't know where they are, and they can't get back up. As soon as they pull up into the cloud, they would start to ice up.

"We got reports from way around the country, as far north as Bella

Coola, about an airplane pawing around at night. They were up and down the valley, trying to find a way out; they didn't know where the hell they where. One guy said he was out hanging a clothesline in the rain and an airplane went by so close, it pretty near knocked him down. As a matter of fact, it wasn't far from there that we found them, near Mount Cheam.

"I guess they got so frustrated and were low on gas, so they take a chance and they headed out to climb through this stuff. They just about missed this bloody peak, pretty near got over it, but they hit the thing and part of the airplane flew over the hump. That's how close it was, a few feet maybe. It started to snow right after, and the wreck got covered over."

The CPA Lodestar had smashed into a mountain slope on Knight Peak, about eleven minutes out of Vancouver. There were no survivors.

Gordie Ballantine had an uneventful flight and arrived safely.

I Think We Found Something

Don's search plane was a de Havilland Rapide, CF-BFP, a twin engine biplane on floats, equipped with long-range fuel tanks. He had been searching for months with no success, and was getting discouraged. All that changed on August 9, 1943.

"I was about ready to give up, because I'd been at it quite a while and I'd been way up the Fraser River, up to the Lillooet area, and coming down the Fraser I thought I'll just go a little bit south. I was going by this mountain that was about seven thousand feet, and I was about six thousand feet, and I spotted this shiny thing. To me it looked like an elevator that had just started to melt out of the snow, and I had a little bit of trouble finding it again. I turned around and came back, and was back and forth a couple of times. The chap that was with me, Bobby Orr, he didn't see it to start with. Finally, we saw it and we got on the radio and contacted Vancouver, and told them we think we found something.

"I went back to Vancouver and got Ted Field, who was the superintendent of flight operations, and my district manager. We flew back and confirmed that it was an airplane. Every day that we went back, a little more of the wreckage popped out of the snow, and then finally the bodies.

"McConachie and Ted Field and a mountain climber friend of Ted's climbed the mountain. They found all the bodies except one, and moved them to a cairn they built. It's still there up on Mount Cheam."

It had taken approximately five hundred hours of flight time, 250,000 square miles, to complete the largest aerial search in the history of the Canadian West. On September 7, 1943, a service was held at the site of the cairn on the summit of Mount William Knight in the Cheam range to pay respect to those lost: Reginald H. Battye, James J. Coyle, Laetitia A. Herron, William G. Holland (first officer), Robert W. Kehr, Ernest W. Kubicek (captain), William N. Scharfe, Rudolph A. Schroeder, Arthur L. Smith, Hugh J. Stewart, Winona M. Stouse, Bernard J. Stouse, and Edna Young (stewardess). Overhead, Ted Field was at the controls of the Rapide. Passing over the crash site, he cut the throttle and nosed into a gentle glide as Don dropped flowers in memory of the unlucky thirteen from the last flight of CF-CPD.

Ted Field and Don Patry load flowers into de Havilland Rapide CF-BFP for memorial ceremony for crash victims, September 7, 1943.
D.V. Patry collection

CHAPTER SIX: ROYAL AIRFORCE FERRY COMMAND

Bombers to Scotland, 1944

In March of 1944, Don moved to Montreal to join the Royal Air Force (RAF) Ferry Command, as a civilian pilot flying bombers over the ocean to Scotland to be used in the war effort against the Germans. He flew B-25s, Lancasters, and DC-3s, which were also known as the C-47. Irene and Ken made the trip from Vancouver by train in April, and the family moved into an apartment. Prior to this, Don was one of four pilots and four radio operators from CPA who were sharing a large old house together.

The check pilot for Ferry Command was a guy by the name of Don McVicker, whom Don knew from Edmonton. "His father was superintendent of the CPR, and when I had that old Fairchild taken out of Dawson Creek by train, he was the boss man on that. I knew Don when he started out as a radio operator for McKenzie Air Service, and he was a pretty smart cookie. He ran a little course on radios and Morse code in the old hangar at Edmonton.

"There was about six of us guys paid him ten bucks every time we went out for a class and he showed us something. I remember I was having some kind of trouble understanding his instructions, and he really chewed me out about being so stupid about this thing, and then I go to the Ferry Command, and by God, he's the check pilot!

"So he checked me out on three or four aircraft: the Lanc, the 3, the Lodestar. The Lodestar was called the Ventura; it was a big Lodestar, but it flew the same as the smaller one. I had a route check with him; we went down to Quebec City in a DC-3 with Cec McNeil. Once I got checked out to his satisfaction, away I went the next day with a B-25.

"The CPR had a whole bunch of B-25's that needed ferrying to the UK and, with CPA being the instigator of the ferry command at that

Ferry Command crew 1944. From back left: Don Patry, Bud Potter,
Cec McNeil. Front left: Bob Phipps, Al Harding, Fred Baron.
Not in photo: captain Ralph Oakes, navigator Harry Hardam.
D.V. Patry collection

time, they said we'll loan you some pilots and radio operators. We used
the air force navigators. When we got down there, it was supposed to
be strictly B-25 Mitchells that we were flying across. The first three were
Mitchells. They were so anxious to get the planes out of Montreal that
even if the weather was only good to Quebec City, why, you'd go. I got
a bit further than Quebec City three or four times, actually.

"We'd go as far as we could and usually we'd get to Gander or
Goose Bay. Then on to Narsarssuak Airbase, Greenland, code name
Bluie West One, locally known as Narshq." Located on the Southwest
coast of Greenland near the village of Narsarsuag, this strategic
airbase's primary purpose was to facilitate patrols of the North Atlantic
shipping lanes and to protect cryolite mines at Ivigut, Greenland, from
German occupation.

Don says, "Narshq was a nicer place to lay over. It had the American
army, and there was PX stores and places to buy stuff. Liquor was

rationed here in Canada and these poor army boys, their tongues were hanging out 'cause there was nothing to drink. I guess it was rationed at these islands, and for a little bottle of booze that cost maybe a buck a bottle, a mickey of gin or scotch, a lot of the guys, they'd take it and sell it. I made a trade for one of those carry-on bags once, but that was about it."

"Sometimes we'd land at Reykjavik, Iceland. We tried to land at the American base, if possible, because of the PX stores. You had to hippity-hop along; the weather had to be real good, because the airplanes didn't have any de-icing equipment on them. They had radios, of course. The navigators, all they had to go by was the sextant, navigating by the stars. They gave us a short course in celestial navigation in Montreal.

"One trip I can remember quite well. I was flying a DC-3 and I had a load of mail and two Liberator crews that belonged to the RAF, based in Nassau, and they were going back home on leave. So I had about ten people altogether, five per crew: a navigator, two pilots, engineers, freight operators, a whole gang. The mail was piled up: there were no seats in the airplane, so they all slept on the mailbags. They were a nice crew; each crew had a leader, and they would come up and say, 'Do you mind if so-and-so comes up for a smoke?' They couldn't smoke back there, because there was two one-hundred gallon round gas tanks beside them!

"Another time in the DC-3 we took off out of Gander; it was snowing, and there was five B-25s getting ready to go. Talking to the weather office man there, he said it was okay to fly out on instruments. These poor RCAF kids that were flying the B-25s, they just didn't know what to do, whether to stay or go, but it was up to them. If they thought they could handle it, why okay. There wasn't any icing conditions mentioned in the cloud and snow, so we took off.

"I had a Norwegian navigator that had been on a binge the night before, and he kept hollering for QTEs (radio transmissions to a radio direction finder station, requesting the bearing of the plane from the station), and we were supposed to be on silent radios. So my first officer, Bill Goodbrand, he had been in the air force but he had some kind of health problem and had been let go, and was flying for CPA and living in the east end of Montreal. He was running a check on where we were going. But this poor navigator, he had this big sextant that none of the other boys had, we were in cloud, and he kept hollering for these QTEs. Bob Phipps was the radio operator, and he'd get these radio bearings. So the navigator got two or three position reports, and sorta made a triangulation out of the thing, and decided we're supposed to be right here. But he kept changing course every time he gave us a reading, and I mean really, really drastic changes, like thirty-five degrees, and that's really something, and we were in cloud all this time.

"We finally broke out of the clouds and then he wanted to shoot the moon. I didn't really know what he was talking about, but instead of getting up in the astrodome, he came running forward to get a shot out the windshield at the front of the plane. Well, he ran right into the windshield and pretty near knocked himself out! In the meantime, we got a bearing on Durnacross, which was a strong beacon that was beamed toward Canada. It was on the north end of Ireland, and the old ADF just went *boom*; it was a class one reading. So Bill says, 'I've got a pretty good track here; you can tell him to sit down,' and Bill took over from there.

"Anyway, when we broke out of the cloud, there was three or four B-25s right on our wingtip! They had followed us through all this, taken off right behind us, and they knew how to fly formation, thank God. You couldn't have your navigation lights on, so we didn't see them, and to this day I don't know how they saw us.

"Because we were in a DC-3, we were slated to go to the Azores, but we had a tailwind that was really blowing, over a hundred knots, and it took us twelve hours from Gander to Prestwick. The Mitchells landed when we got closer in; they knew where they were by that time. We never talked to them, and I don't think they ever knew we changed our minds from going to the Azores to going direct."

Another flight also had some brief excitement provided by traffic, except this time instead of being off the wing, the company was at sea level. "We broke out of cloud one day and there was a convoy of ships on the water below. You were supposed to have a Very flare gun and shoot the colour of the day so they could recognize you, and know that you weren't the enemy. Anyway, we got this gun out and there was a place on the side of the airplane you could push the barrel into and pull the trigger. I'm sure we shot the wrong colour, but they didn't bother us; we didn't get shot at."

The crews were housed in military barracks for layovers, but they were not all treated the same, which caused Don some discomfort. His usual crew was first officer Bill Goodbrand and radio operator Bob Phipps. The Canadian attitude was that while they had different roles when flying the plane, they were a team, and once on the ground there was little need for distinctions between captain and the other positions. However, this would not do in the RAF environment, where rank and the chain of command were essential to maintain order and appearance. Consequently, to his embarrassment, Don was treated as an officer and the rest of the crew was treated more or less like buck privates.

The trip back to Canada was not anticipated with much enthusiasm. The crews went back as passengers, or perhaps more accurately, freight, on BOAC planes.

"I didn't mind too much coming back in the Liberators, except for a couple of times when we had to sit in the seats. The bomb bay was better, because it had mattresses and sleeping bags. Cec McNeil and his crew and my crew always tried to get on the airplane first so we could grab the bomb bay. There would be Thermoses of hot coffee hung up on the racks, and you could also get into the cockpit if you wanted."

It was sort of a slap-happy outfit; the cockpit door was a piece of plywood hung on with bungee cords. The minute the BOAC pilots got near clouds, instead of trying to find a lower layer, they started to climb. We called this getting over the BOAC mountains. They'd get way up there, seventeen thousand, eighteen thousand feet. At that height we needed oxygen, but didn't always have it. Most of the guys would just fall asleep."

One time on the way back, we had two crews in the bomb bay, and everybody grabbed a coffee. We had a bottle of rum with us, so we put a bit in our coffee and then we all went to sleep as they started to climb. I wasn't quite asleep yet, and one of the crew came out to tell us to put the oxygen masks on. He was wearing a mask that was one of those green bags that when you breathed, it puffed way up. I didn't know what it was coming out of the cockpit; I guess between the rum and the lack of oxygen, we were pretty happy, and we just laughed at him and didn't pay too much attention. He gave up and went back up in the cockpit, and I don't think we ever put our masks on. Anyway, we fell asleep and didn't wake up until we were coming into Montreal."

Rations

In contrast to the hardships experienced in Vancouver during the war years, and to Irene's surprise, rationing was not much of an issue in Montreal. In fact, she would occasionally make up packages of food to send overseas. One time Don got a request from the customs agent in Prestwick, who was longing for oranges, fresh eggs, and ham. So Irene put together a parcel, and it went on the next trip. However, just like the eggs and oranges of the Muskwa River adventure, there were delivery problems.

"I couldn't find the customs guy, and we were turning right around to head back home. As a matter of fact, there was a Lib sitting there ready to go back, and I still had this bundle of stuff. So there was a little Scotsman there that accepted the airplanes when you landed, handled the paperwork, and signed that it was delivered in one piece. He was a nice guy, so I asked him if he would like the food. He was about to go home on leave and was thankful to get it.

On a later trip, he thanked me again and said that his mother had been sickly, and she had really appreciated the package, as she hadn't had a fresh egg in ages."

Air Conditioned B-25

"They had airplanes stashed away in Norfolk, Virginia, at the navy base, and Bill Goodbrand and I and Bob Phipps were to bring one back to Montreal. We went with three other crews in a DC-3 to Norfolk. We found our plane, and it had been sitting out on the field there for a while, but it was supposed to be serviced and ready to go.

"I begin starting the engines up, and they just sorta puked water out the exhaust pipes. Finally, they got running pretty good, and we were able to take off. We just got out over the water, and *whoosh*, away went the top hatch. It hadn't been locked. All the maps and any loose stuff just blew right out. Well, we had to go back.

"We had those throat mikes, and poor old Bill, he's working the radio, trying to talk to the tower, saying that we've lost the top of the airplane. The engines in the B-25s (Wright R-2600, 1,700-horsepower) had short little exhaust stacks, and they were right beside you and you could hardly hear. Bill was trying to talk above all this noise and rushing air, and I could see the veins in his neck popping out; I thought he was going to have a stroke.

"So we get on the ground and go to another airplane that was sitting there, take the top off it, put it on our plane, and away we go. The route back took us right over New York, and I remember it was quite a chore getting through there, because they had air traffic controllers, which we didn't have in Canada. In those days, we just talked to the tower. We got back to Montreal, and it's snowing like mad and we have to do a let down. At the same time, a BOAC plane is coming in. The BOAC pilots could fly instruments but they didn't like to, so these guys let down way out to see if they could get underneath the cloud. So we're going down through the snow and the poor guy in the tower, we could tell him that we'd gone over the range and our altitude, but he really didn't know where either of us were, and he was getting a little excited." Both planes landed without any problem, but the situation illustrated the importance of air traffic control.

"The BOAC pilots tended to be older guys, used to flying VFR. Lots of pilots used to VFR had difficulty adjusting to instruments, and some never did. For me, flying contact for so long through valleys and up rivers, I think it made you a better instrument pilot, because when you did get into conditions where the visibility was low, once you got the hang of instruments, you sort of knew what to expect."

After the Germans surrendered in 1945, the RAF Ferry Command ceased operations. The Command had delivered an incredible 9027 aircraft over the North Atlantic, a significant accomplishment considering the distance, the weather, and the rudimentary navigational equipment that the crews relied on.

The Patrys left Montreal by train, destined for Vancouver, on a hot Dominion Day weekend in July 1944, detouring to Edmonton along the way to visit family. Don had his job with CPA waiting for him, and he was ready to pick up where he had left off. But unbeknownst to him, conditions at CPA had changed in a big way.

Winds of Change at CPA, 1944

When Don returned to Vancouver in July 1944, he found the atmosphere at CPA had changed drastically. For starters, the company had decided that pilots of airlines amalgamated into CPA would have their seniority based on the date they had started flying with the original company, not the date they joined CPA. Since a good number of these pilots had flown for years, Don found himself bumped down the list. This was discouraging, and caused tension.

There were also political influences at work undermining CPA. Clarence Decatur Howe was a powerful minister in the governments of prime ministers Mackenzie King and Louis St. Laurent. Known as the Minister of Everything, he directed Canada's industrial war effort in World War Two. "C.D. Howe had made up his mind that TCA was going to be the only airline in Canada, and CPA was breaking up—they were going back to bush flying. There was a bunch of pilots junior to me who were going to be let go, and CPA was turning them over to the military. Well, there was no fighting left anymore; the war was practically over, so some of them ended up in uniform as foot soldiers.

"The whole scene had changed there, which contributed to us leaving. I talked to Grant and he said, 'I have nothing to offer you; you'd better go with TCA,' and anytime I wanted to come back, I was welcome.

"CPA survived that crisis which, it turned out, became typical for them. I flew until November 1945, and then I had to quit to get on with TCA. We had a lot of friends in CPA and, as a matter of fact, when Pacific Western Airlines (PWA) bought CPA in 1987, they had a wake for CPA out in Vancouver. We were invited, and everybody was wearing black arm bands. There was a few guys out there that wanted to know what we were doing there. So Stan Emery, an old friend of ours, he says, 'Well, if it wasn't for Smoke, here, you wouldn't have a job, and that's why he's here!'

"Anyway, in 1946 we thought we'd come east for a year, and then put a bid in on a route out west with TCA and go back to Vancouver. Well, it's 2003 and we're still here."

Trans Canada Airways

After making the difficult decision to leave CPA, Don struck an agreement with Herb Seagram of TCA. He would come over to TCA, take the required two months of ground school training beginning January 1, 1946, in Winnipeg, fly as first officer only as long as it took to learn the routes and routines, and then he would fly left seat. There were no guarantees, of course, but if he passed the muster, that was the deal.

The ground school was a little risky, inasmuch as you could be drummed out in the blink of an eye if you got on the wrong side of an instructor. Don had no problem until the end of the course, when he

had to fly the simulator while being evaluated by one of the more difficult instructors, who seemed to think that student failures were his successes. In any event, Don neglected to descend prior to landing, and the instructor stormed off, saying he would have to repeat the test at a later date. Waiting, however, was the last thing Don wanted to do, so he grabbed one of the other instructors and repeated the test with no problem. To his surprise, upon exiting the simulator, he saw the original instructor, who,

D.V. Patry, Trans Canada Airlines, 1946.
D.V. Patry collection

true to his nature asked, "Why didn't you do that the first time?" Don's reply was succinct and completely devoid of tact: "If you hadn't been sitting beside me, I would have!"

Like most people early in a career, Don was more concerned with the present than the future, and he didn't appreciate the impact on seniority that changing jobs would have. "Seniority didn't mean very much to me in those days, and when I moved, I had to start at the bottom of the list. I lost a good six years, not being able to bring CPA service into TCA."

Three other CPA pilots were on the same training course: Bill Boyes, George Gilmore, and Stan Seaton. Once in Toronto, they all boarded in the top floor of a rooming house near St. Clair Avenue. Although all three were married, their wives had stayed behind until housing arrangements were made. In 1946 Toronto had a severe shortage of accommodation. After a lot of searching, the only place Don could find was a duplex in the village of Belfountain, a long drive north of the airport, but it would have to do.

Irene was staying in Edmonton with Ken and baby daughter Jeanne (Judy), who had joined the family through adoption in June 1945. As soon as they heard the news about their new home, they packed up and got on the train for Toronto. Unfortunately, by the time they arrived, the rental arrangements had fallen through and left them in quite a predicament. After considerable and somewhat frantic searching, they bought an unfurnished, partially completed two-bedroom bungalow in Longbranch, an area of Toronto now known as Etobicoke. The basement had two rooms, a toilet, and a laundry tub. The main floor had two bedrooms and a bathroom with a tub. Furnishing the house proved to be a challenge for Irene. "This is 1946. You can't for love nor money buy a stove or fridge or beds; there was nothing available, and we had brought a bare minimum with us. I remember going to Simpson's at Young and Queen, and there was no furniture on the floor. A trolley came through these swinging doors carrying a chesterfield, and a guy standing there immediately said,

'I'll buy it,' and it was gone. We had a card table to eat on, and an old electric hot plate to cook with."

Things got even more interesting in Long Branch, as Bill Boyes, his wife Marie, and their young child moved in with the Patrys until they could secure their own housing. George Gilmore also moved in temporarily. And Don's niece, Vivian, from Edmonton moved in. So Irene had a full and busy household, to say the least. "So there we have three men in uniform coming and going at all hours of the day and night, three women, and three kids, and nobody could figure out who belonged to whom! It's hot, and there's no refrigerator, so George built an icebox out of crates and we bought ice from the local iceman. We got a proper stove and fridge eventually."

In July 1946 Don was back in Winnipeg to take the TCA training required to fly left seat. It seemed to work, as Captain D.V. Patry would fly with TCA for the next twenty-nine years.

Flying The Line With TCA

Don's first route was Toronto–Winnipeg, a routine trip in a DC-3. Before long, however, he was being checked out on flights to Chicago and New York, and he wasn't keen on this new development.

"I didn't want to fly those runs, because I'd heard tales of them stacking 'em up eight and ten planes, and when one guy lands, you drop down one thousand feet, and down, and down, until finally it's your turn to land. By then it's really closed in, and if you have to pull up, well, holy smokes, everything goes haywire.

"Anyway, I had to do a route check with them, and write a little exam, and draw all the range stations, the altitudes for different quadrants right down into New York and La Guardia. They had an NDB out in the middle of an inlet; you'd crowd over this beacon and have to hold and keep your altitude up. The Viscounts were pressurized, so you'd be up seventeen or eighteen thousand feet, and they might let you down to twelve, but there'd be ten airplanes below you. You'd do your procedure turn, go out and back and off to the leg again; it was just a racetrack, round and round. You know there'd be an airplane one thousand feet right below you in the clouds, and all you could see was these blinking lights going by, and it looked like they were right there! The guy at the bottom would get clearance to land, so you'd hold your breath, because if he didn't get in, you didn't get in. Before long, I got used to the New York run, and it didn't bother me anymore.

"There were two good cycles, New York and Chicago. The tower operators at Chicago were good. It was a busy, busy airport. Two parallel runways and you'd be going in and gosh, just off your wingtip would be another airplane. When you talked on the radio, you just gave your flight number and they came right back and told you what to do. Later, when they got radar, they gave you vectors.

"Either cycle was two trips a day. An early morning flight, sit there for an hour or so, back to TO [Toronto], sit for an hour, go again, and back home. We did that for three days and then had five days off. One of those days you were on twenty-four-hour reserve; it didn't matter if it was the middle of the night or day. By seven o'clock in the evening, you figure I'm not going to have to go up, then *boom*, they call you. When we first moved to Port Credit, we couldn't get a phone, and they'd send a bloody taxi out for you. Not to pick you up, just to tell you to go in to work!

"All flying time for an aircraft for a month was organized in a block. At the end of every month, you'd bid for the block you wanted. Some had more time off; some had more hours and more money. You bid your choices one, two, three, four, whatever your seniority was. Then you found out what your flying conditions would be for the month. You tried to get Christmas off, and so did everyone else. The blocks really determined your salary, so there was a lot of competition, and you finagled these blocks as best you could.

"You usually flew with the same first officer for a month, so you'd get to know these boys. Then there was the odd captain that nobody wanted to fly with. One of the guys, Harold Twitchell, developed a scheme that had the captains bid first and then the blocks would come out; that way, the first officers could try and bid around this miserable guy. We called it the Twitchell bid.

"In the DC-3, I just couldn't get the seat down far enough to be comfortable, and it had a bungee rig on the back to hold up the heavy seat, and I always unhooked it. Then the next guy after me couldn't get the damn seat up and they'd have to call a mechanic! The mechanics got to know that I had the seat as low as it would go, and they'd get in and see me and say, 'Oh God, here's old Smoke; I guess I gotta put that bungee back on!'

"Holidays were not in the vocabulary in the early days. On the Northstar, I think it was seventy-five hours you had to put in per month. More than that was fine, but you didn't get any extra time off, and if you got under seventy-five, you'd have to make it up in the next block.

"CPA had good maintenance crews and so did TCA. TCA would start out with a new airplane and I don't know why, but they'd tear it apart and half the things they didn't need to do. The Vanguard had miles and miles of wiring, and at the start the engines on that thing only lasted about ten hours. Something was always going haywire. The compressors used to blow up and come out the side of the engine, so they had to strap those things with heavy jackets so they wouldn't come out in chunks. Eventually, they got things figured out, and the engines lasted fine.

"The Vanguard was a British plane and they used different hydraulic oil, but TCA had to change the bloody hydraulic fluid to one that was designed for fire protection; it was slower burning. That was a good idea, except this new hydraulic oil chewed up the O-rings and eventually they had to change the whole set, and there was thousands of them. Those poor mechanics.

"The Vanguard had a complicated feathering system for the props, and it was a big prop on a little engine. If the prop started to run away, there were clamps around the prop shaft that would sort of plop out and stop it. That could also be dangerous, because if it stopped too quick, why, it would just twist the engine out of its mount. So they had to change that.

"One time coming back from Montreal, the props got out of sync really bad, and I didn't know what was going on. So I throttled back a little bit and pulled the rpm back, and finally it smoothed out. I never did find out what was wrong with those engines.

"Another time, we were in cloud going into Chicago with the de-icing on, as we were icing up. The stewardess came up front and said, 'There's something going on back here; there's sparks flying!' I go back and, sure enough, you could see it sparking in the tail end. When we landed, it looked like we'd been hit by lightning. A short in the tail feathers had burnt right through the leading edge of the fin and the elevator."

The Viscount
"The pilot's seats were up off the floor on a hump at the front of the cabin, and when you stepped in, you got up on a platform, and then your feet were sort of dangling in mid-air. The steering control was a series of universal joints and rods with little steering wheels on either side. You couldn't move the thing without it jerking, and my check ride reports always said the same thing: 'Rough on the nose wheel steering.' Of course they had to say something, and that was always it.

"The training to fly a new type of plane was usually a month long and held in Montreal. Then you had to have a checkout every six months. They'd do route checks unannounced, and when you got back, you'd have a little lecture. I wasn't very good at knowing where the hell everything was in the cabin, for example. I knew where it was my way, which was not always what the book said, one, two, three, that sort of thing. When I knew I was going to have a check ride, Irene and I would go through the manuals, and she would quiz me. As a matter of fact, to this day she still recalls the question on automatic decompression!

"You never knew in advance about route checks, and you just had to be prepared. Your medical was every six months, with a thorough medical every two years by the company doctor.

"The Viscount simulator was really the first one that we had. It was sort of a chain and universal joint set-up with a million gears and chains wrapped around it, and it was a rough thing. Eventually, it got that you did all of your groundwork in the simulator, but you still had to have a route check."

The DC-8

"The Vanguard was the last prop job I flew for the company, and in 1964 I started on the DC-8. They had them in 1960, but I couldn't get on them. They were the pride and joy of the airline, and boy, you had to be somebody to fly the 8! You bid to fly new aircraft, knowing your seniority and knowing what the conditions might be. If you really wanted on an aircraft, you might bid on it even if it meant being on reserve all month.

"Being sort of a junior on the 8, I got blocks that were all mixed up: fly out to Vancouver and maybe lay over, or maybe back to Toronto for a day and then over to London or Frankfurt or Vienna. Then add the odd charter to Nassau or Jamaica. You'd get a charter flight over to Zurich or Munich, but they weren't very nice flights, because you'd have to deadhead someplace and pick up another trip. You were gone for days, and your time didn't seem to mean anything to the company in those days.

"Say you had a delay taking off in Toronto. You'd hang around and hang around and be told the airplane would be ready any minute, and finally you'd get going to Glasgow about three hours late. Then you'd deadhead to some other place to pick up a flight, a lot of wasted time and you didn't get paid for sitting on the ground. You just had to keep going; there was nobody else to take the airplane. Deadheading wasn't that tiresome, but you usually didn't do any sleeping in the meantime. You could be up for twenty-four hours and then get in an airplane and fly it.

"The DC-8s were half freighter—when you got up front, it was just a narrow aisle between shipping crates. The passengers were in the back, and the freight was between the pilot and passengers. It was sort of a crummy thing. We had a men's room up front, but there was no curtains or anything on it. Once a couple of stewardesses came up and here's the first officer sitting on the can!

"To get to the cockpit, you had to lift up a little door and practically get down on your hands and knees to get through, and all the while the passengers are sitting right there watching you. I remember going back one time, and the passengers were startled to see the captain climbing out of this trap door.

"The 8s were well equipped auto pilots that really worked, tied in with the inertial navigation system (INS). These had three very expensive gyros, which we used for navigating. The second officer had to be in the airplane a good hour and a half ahead of time and set up the coordinates, and when the captain got in the cockpit, he had to check each one. When I first went on the 8s, we had navigators. They used the INS, but not exclusively; they did a lot of celestial work too.

"There was four of us in the cockpit: the navigator, the second officer, the first officer, and the captain. I used to smoke cigars at that time, and the cockpit would get pretty smoky. When they cleaned out the air filters, they'd be yellow. If I had a cigar, why, the rest of them wanted one too. I guess I started quite a few people smoking cigars, but it was mostly mine they smoked, and there was a few complaints, so I quit.

"I hand-flew the airplane until we got to our cruising altitude, which you never got to right off the bat. Depending on the load, you often had to step climb, fly at one level until you'd burnt enough fuel to climb again. We'd be out of Canada before getting up around thirty thousand feet. The separation was two thousand feet vertical and you had ninety nautical miles each side, so you could wander around a bit, which was a good thing because there was the odd navigator that got a little bit out of his way."

"I didn't have too much excitement on the 8; they were usually good flights. I never had any trouble passengers—well, maybe a couple of times. In those days, I'd go back and talk to the guy and try to calm him down, and I'd say you better come up front with me and see what's going on up there. They'd come up and settle down, and that would be the end of it. Once in the Viscount days, the Prince of Thailand came up and sat in the first officer's seat. He was a pilot himself and got quite a kick out of it."

"I had to fly for one hundred hours with a check pilot on the 8. There was two check pilots, Bill Benson and Jack Smith. They were like two mother hens. They flew as first officer, Bill one trip, Jack the next. Bill was on one of my last route check flights from Vienna; we were coming in the north route. Between Greenland and Goose Bay, the oil pressure dropped on one engine, and we had to shut it down. If you lost the oil, eventually the engine would seize up on you. By that time, we had used up a lot of fuel and the airplane was pretty light—I think it picked up speed. We came all the way into Toronto on three engines with no problem.

"We were coming out of Miami one night during a strike by the air traffic controllers, who were working to rule. It was dark and we had just reached our cruising altitude, around twenty-eight thousand feet, when they came on the radio and said that the Miami tower had got a call that there was a bomb onboard the aircraft. That sort of sends a shiver up your neck.

"It was a dirty night, with thunderstorms all around, and we were directly north of Tampa. I called the centre and said we have a bomb scare, turn us to the nearest airport. I closed the throttle, did a 180, started down, and never touched the throttle until we could see the field in Tampa. We landed, and it was raining like mad, and they taxied us way out in the boondocks, and to get a ramp up to the airplane in that particular spot, they had to get permission from somebody in Tampa to cross a certain road! Well, we had to get people off the airplane, so we just popped the chutes out and I left one of the engines running to keep the lights up.

"The passengers went down the chutes, except for one guy with a wooden leg, and he refused to get on that chute. The second officer was a big Army boy; he'd flown helicopters. He just grabbed him by the seat of the pants and shoved him out. The guy slid down the chute with his wooden leg stuck up in the air! The only injury was a lady who broke her little finger. When they got down, it was still raining like mad, so they went under the wing! I don't know what they were thinking, because I'd told them about the bomb threat. Eventually, taxis came out and got the passengers. I stayed on board, talking to the tower, trying to get the ramp out there, and finally they brought it out. The baggage was all taken even further out into the boondocks and checked over. They didn't find any bomb, and we taxied the plane back to the terminal building and the passengers reboarded, except for four who wouldn't get back on. I can't remember if the man with the wooden leg was one of them or not."

Two Generations

"I flew two months together with my son Ken, not consecutively, but over two blocks. After getting his licence, he had tried to get on with Air Canada, but was told he was a quarter-inch too short of the standard, and they turned him down. So he went with CPA and just nicely got on permanent, and then all of a sudden the phone's ringing and now Air Canada can't get along without him. I don't know if they thought he grew, or they changed the regulation. Actually, I think it was the result of a kind of accidental conversation I had with K.J. Davis—he was one of the top guys in Air Canada. When he asked about Ken and was told he was with CPA, his only comment was, 'Well, we've got to do something about that.'

"So Ken had to decide to stay or go, history repeating itself. He really liked the west coast, and it was a bit of a dilemma. So he went and talked to Harvey Johnston, who was Superintendent of Flight Operations in Vancouver. Harv said go with TCA, there's more opportunity there. Ken had to quit CPA before he could be interviewed, and ended up retiring from Air Canada as captain in 2001.

"One time going into Vancouver with Ken in the 8, we had a fire warning in the number two engine. The bells started ringing and the red lights went on. So we went through the procedure of shutting it down. There were two systems for engines, and we used them both, and the light finally went out. It turned out to be a short in the wiring and there was no fire, but of course we didn't know that until later."

Last Flight

"On my last flight in July 1975, we were coming back from Zurich into Montreal, and it was raining and really gusty. That old airplane just greased on, and after taxiing in, I went upstairs in the terminal building and here's the whole family: Irene, Ken, Judy, my niece Vivian, grandkids Stuart and Vanessa, friends from Vancouver, Air Canada officials. I was real surprised. So they took a bunch of pictures and got on board the flight to Toronto.

"It was clear coming into Toronto, and we're letting down and a friend of mine, Bill Boyes, is sitting out at the end of runway 23 for takeoff, heading to Frankfurt. So he's nattering away at me, and then the tower got in on the act, seeing as how this is my last flight. I'm doing a back course onto 23, and at that time there was no ILS (Instrument Landing System) on the back part. I had everything all lined up, and boy, it was just coming down nice. There wasn't a burble in the airplane, and I'm just about ready to land, and somebody said something just as I started to round out, and we dropped onto the runway. On the 8, as soon as a wheel started to turn, the spoilers popped out and it just wasn't gonna fly anymore."

Don on his final flight with
Air Canada, June 12, 1975.
D.V. Patry collection

DC-8 #863, last plane flown by Don for Air Canada.
D.V. Patry collection

A bumpy landing could not overshadow a remarkable thirty-eight-year professional flying career, from the humble beginning with one passenger in a Cirrus Moth flying at 90 MPH over Alberta wheatfields, to captain of a DC-8 with two hundred passengers cruising at 500 MPH over the Atlantic Ocean.

CHAPTER EIGHT: **AFTER THE AIRLINES**

Eagle Lake

As Don approached retirement, he began searching for a piece of property on a lake that could accommodate an airstrip and a float base, a rather tall order. Following a lead from a real estate agent, Don and Irene met a man by the name of Bob Bishop, who had recently taken ownership of Sir Sam's Inn on Eagle Lake in Haliburton, Ontario. Bob had put in a seventeen-hundred-foot airstrip between Eagle Lake and Moose Lake to attract potential buyers for cottage lots on Eagle Lake. Bob had got his pilot's licence some time earlier, but had not flown much since. When he found out that Don had an airplane, a deal was soon struck, and he traded a lot on the lake for the Tripacer, MIB. The Patrys became the first purchasers of a lot on Eagle Lake in the fall of 1966, and started construction on a retirement home the next spring.

Part of the deal was that Don was to check Bob out on MIB. "He turned out to be a good pilot. He hadn't flown a plane with a control wheel or flaps or wheels. He'd learned to fly on skis and floats in a PA-12. I rode around with him for awhile and told him this is a little short field, go over to Muskoka and make a few landings on the long strip where you have time to think about going around again. Oh yeah, he'd do that; I think the minute we left the strip, he was doing circuits and he nearly got his feet wet a couple of times! He went on and got a 182, and eventually developed the ski hill there."

Bob built a hangar and things seemed ideal for a few years. Unfortunately, once it had fulfilled its purpose of attracting aviation enthusiast buyers, the airstrip that had been guaranteed to stay became too valuable to remain. Spoken promises are ephemeral and the romance of the grass strip was lost to the economics of real estate development. Any planes at Eagle Lake would now have to be on floats.

After the Tripacer came a Cessna 180 on floats, CF-MDC. This was

Don and Piper Tripacer MIB.
D.V. Patry collection

probably Don's favourite airplane. The plan was that after he retired, Don would lease out himself and the 180, so he formed a company called Patry Air Lease. The company also leased out snowmobiles until they "very shortly found out that leasing snowmobiles is a losing proposition, because nobody looks after them and it's just a matter of maintenance, maintenance, maintenance." Before long, Don would discover that the economics of aircraft leasing weren't any better.

One-Plane Airline

It was the fall of 1973, and a hunting outfitter by the name of Tom Wilson in Gowganda, Ontario, was looking to lease an airplane. So Don, Irene, and niece Viv and her husband Bert Meeker flew up to check things out. They found a well-run business that included Wilson's mother. Don agreed to lease MDC to them, on the condition that the only pilots would be Tom Wilson or his employee, a young fellow by the name of Mark Davis.

"This young lad Davis, his father was an airline pilot, and I had

Cessna 180 on floats, CF-MDC. Of the airplanes he owned, this was Don's favourite.
D.V. Patry collection

confidence in him. He wanted to get on with TCA, and he got word from the company to come in for an interview. He was pretty sure that he would get on, but it was right at the peak of hunting season, and Tom wouldn't let him go. Well, he was pretty upset about this, so he just left. Tom was in a bind, and he hired this guy that had been flying a desk in the air force all his life, and had very little float experience. I didn't know it, but he got the job of flying MDC. Our agreement on who was to fly my plane was based on a handshake; I had nothing in writing."

Irene got the phone call. "So Don's away on a flight, and on Thanksgiving Day, I get a phone call. 'Mrs. Patry, this is Tom Wilson, and I have some bad news. We just sunk your airplane.' In a landlocked lake, I might add."

For Don, the only good news was that nobody was hurt in the accident. "It was a windy, windy day, and this guy went in to pick up a party at this lake with a little island in the middle. He tried to land in the lee of the island and he overshot, and as he popped out the other side, a gust caught him just as he was about to land, tipped him over, and he dug a wing tip in. Then the airplane was on its back with the floats sticking up. The people to be picked up had a boat right there, and they went out and picked the guy up. He was kinda wet."

Irene was pragmatic about the mishap, but she understood Don's attachment to MDC. "They went in and inspected the plane; it should have been written off, but it was Don's baby. It was insured, and after Don talked to the adjustor, he figured he could rebuild it on budget with the insurance payout. So it was taken out by helicopter to Sudbury, then trucked to a shop in Oshawa to be repaired. It was in there all winter and on into July. Don was going down there to check on it and kept asking if the insurance money was going to cover the costs, and the answer was always sure, sure. Well, when it's ready, there's six thousand dollars owing on it, and the guy won't release it until he's paid! So things got a little touchy for a while."

Don consulted a lawyer, who gave it to him straight. "He told me, 'Smoke, nobody wins on this thing; the only people that'll make any money are the lawyers. Settle it out of court and take your lumps!' So I talked to the guy, and we cut the bill down to four thousand dollars.

"I got the airplane home, but gosh, there was an awful lot of work yet to be done. There was mud behind the panel that hadn't been cleaned out, and it wasn't insulated properly. I was perturbed at the job they did on the headliner. The rest was a pretty good job, but still, I worked on it for a full year before I felt comfortable in it. The next thing you know, the government comes calling, wanting to know why this company is all expenses and no income. They went through the books and decided we were legit, but by this time, we decided that Patry Air Lease wasn't such a good idea and wound it down."

Just For the Fun of It
Don retired from Air Canada in July 1975. Now, instead of flying hundreds of passengers across the country in a DC-8, he flew just two in the 180 on floats—Irene and their eight-year-old grandson Stuart— back out west, ending up in Kelowna, BC. "We had this book from the

government showing the float facilities, but the information was so out of date, there was no facilities where they thought they were. Anyway, we got out and back no problem."

In the fall of 1975, Don was hired to fly for Lorne Turcotte at Gogama, and Irene found herself once again in a cabin in the bush. "Bush flying, a trip down memory lane. We had a little cabin with a tiny stove. I didn't mind, no housework: you just opened the door and swept out the dirt. It was fine."

Don was flying a 185 that belonged to a friend by the name of Don Beatty. The next spring, he flew his 180, MDC, up for the fishing season and again in the fall for hunting. "That was a dirty fall. The lake was freezing over and it was windy and snowy; you'd get up in the morning and there'd be six inches of snow on the airplane. I was glad to see the end of the season. It was cold and I went in to pick up two hunters on this little island. There was a dock, and hidden underneath was a big pointed rock. It was fine and dandy as long as you didn't put any weight on the airplane. I didn't know that.

"The first trip in, it was blowing snow, and the water was really rough. I taxied up to this dock and they piled a bunch of stuff in the airplane. The back seat was out and the compartment was lined with plastic. One of the things that went in was an outboard motor, and I had to put it in on its head, but the skeg was right close to the back window. With the rocking of the airplane, and one thing and another, it went up against the window and broke it.

"The second trip I went back in to pick the second guy up, and he was a big guy. I didn't have as much stuff to carry, so the plane was lighter, but he jumped off this dock onto the float, and it went down and the rock punctured it. I didn't realize this, but I did think that I had a heck of a time getting off. It was rough, but I finally got it up in the air, got back to the base, and that was it for the day.

"The next morning, I went out and here, the poor old airplane, the wing tip is pretty near in the water. The only thing I could guess was that the fuel had all gone to one side. I never shut the main fuel cock off, so the fuel could go from one wing to the other depending on how it was sitting, but there was never much gas in that airplane. In those days, you just had enough to get there and back again, five gallons at the very most, so it can't be that. I opened the step float first, and God, the water was right there.

"I pumped it out and made a few flights, but in the meantime, it was so cold that the oil congealed in the oil cooler. I thought I warmed it up enough, but I guess not, because the cooler cracked and I had oil splattered all over. That was the last trip, and I pulled it up out of the water and it was supposed to go in Lorne's hangar over winter. I went up in the spring with Chris Minto to get my airplane, and here it had sat outside all winter. I patched the float, put on a rebuilt oil cooler, and flew the bloody thing home, and that was it. Been there, done that, not doing it anymore.

"A second, short-lived career in bush flying. It was not a very successful venture, as I paid for all repairs. But I guess I made as much money as I did the first time around, which was nothing. Just for the fun of it!"

BJS Rises from the Ashes

It takes a great deal of determination to rebuild an old, worn-out airplane, and the rougher the condition, the more impressive the feat. So when Don heard that PRA's old biplane, Waco CF-BJS, had been taken on as a project by Air Canada captain Gerry Norbert, he was very impressed. Rightly so, as BJS had been subjected to a crash, a forest fire, and half a century in the bush.

"I'm not sure, but I think Dal picked that plane up at the Lakehead. The last time I flew it was about 1938. It had a 330 Jacobs engine and a fixed pitch prop on it. You could take the back seat out and use it as a freighter. I don't know if Peace River Airways lost it or sold it, but it wound up being flown into Yellowknife again and out on the west coast. Fifty-one years ago, somebody was flying it up to Watson Lake and the engine quit just before Watson Lake, and he put it in the trees.

"Apparently, it wasn't hurt real bad, but it was hung up in the trees and a forest fire came along and burned the trees, and it fell down and did more damage. This Gerry fellow's an old airplane buff, and he flew out of Watson Lake and had heard about this crash. Anyway, he ended up buying BJS from Dal's estate, sight unseen, for a dollar. Eventually, someone approached him, wanting to buy it, and Gerry thought he should at least take a look before he sold, so he flew over and found it not too far from the Alaska Highway. So he decided to rebuild it himself. Took him four trips with a helicopter to get it out to the nearest road, and then it was trucked to Watson Lake.

The fuselage was in pretty bad shape, and there was one float that could be rebuilt, but that's about it." In the fall of 2003, Gerry and retired Air Canada captain Al McLeod went to Kansas to retrieve a Waco fuselage for parts. BJS is now in Winnipeg, being slowly rebuilt by Gerry.

Old Don's Toy and Other Planes

Before long, Don decided that the extra work and bother of changing back and forth between wheels and floats was something he could live without. "I sold MDC to a guy in Sudbury and started looking for a plane on wheels; we were out of the float business."

After a brief search, Don located a Piper Cherokee 140. "The 140, ODT [Old Don's Toy], came from Collingwood. Joe Kane was the chief mechanic for John Worts, who owned the airport, and he told me this plane was for sale. It was Mrs. Worts' airplane and had at one time been used by a flying school, so it had a lot of time on it, but it was all fixed up, instrument equipped. It didn't have rear seats, so I got a couple secondhand and installed them."

After parting with his beloved 180, Don found that other planes were a hard act to follow. "I never really liked that plane, and I didn't have it long, and I sold it back to the people I got it from. Shortly after, it got busted up at the new field at Barrie, the one before Oro."

The next plane was a Cessna 140, CF-FPM, purchased from Karen

A Cessna 140 that Don owned after retiring.
D.V. Patry collection

Smith. "This was the one that she had all rebuilt and had flown up to the Arctic. After a while, I sold it to David Fisher and Dwayne Richie."

Don and Ken took on a rebuilding project in 1982 with the purchase of a Stinson 108-3, C-GCRL. "We bought it from a CPA pilot who lived at the Guelph Air Park. He was going to rebuild it, but got involved in another project and wanted to sell. We trucked it up to Barrie and put it in Ken's garage. The air had to be let out of the tires to get it in. We did the wings and fuselage, and Ken installed the engine. Then in late 1983 we put a trailer hitch on the tail wheel spring and towed it over to a heated hangar at Collingwood, where we did a lot more work, including painting.

"We got it finished and it was a nice airplane, but by this time we had one too many planes. Ken had the 195 and I had bought a 172, so we sold the Stinson to Lloyd Windh. A few years ago at Osh Kosh, we saw CRL sitting there with Yankee registration on it. So we went over and asked what they wanted for it. They said $48,000 US. We had sold it for $23,000 Canadian."

Stinson 108-3, C-GCRL.
D.V. Patry collection

CHAPTER NINE: **ONE MORE TRIP**

Don ended up buying a Cessna 172, c-gbry, from a member of the Brampton Flying Club. "It was a nice airplane but was under-powered, loaded up with gas, and two people it was a dog. Anyway, I wanted to fly one more trip across the country to Edmonton. We went down through the States. Near Duluth it was raining like mad, and we managed to get into a little airport about a mile from the big airport, but almost flipped the plane over. When we left there, I thought I heard something, but it cleared up. We kept going and just past the international field, it started to run rough and we did a 180, but it cleared up again, so we headed west.

"By six o'clock that evening, we landed at a place called Wolf Point, Montana, fueled up, and just got in the air, and boy, that old engine let loose and was shaking like crazy, so we came around and landed and taxied up to one of the hangars. We couldn't see anybody and weren't sure what we were going to do, but at least we were on the ground.

"Before long, a fellow by the name of Lorne French came out. He and his wife had a crop dusting operation and had just put his plane away for the day. He asked what the problem was, and I said I didn't know, but the engine's not running right. So he opened the hangar doors and said, 'Let's see what we can do.'

"We took a compression test, and it was right up and we couldn't figure that out, so we did a static test and one cylinder was just flat. We turned the prop over and found that it was the number one cylinder, and when we took the top off, the tappets just fell off in our hands. So we knew what was wrong."

Lorne told Don to call a friend of his in Billings, who ran an airplane salvage operation, and mention his name. "I phoned this fellow and it turned out that he drank a bit, so the conversation was a little confusing, but I finally got it through to him that I needed a cylinder

A Cessna 172 C-GBRY that Don flew for his last "big" trip.
D.V. Patry collection

for a continental engine. He said he had one that he could ship that night and it would cost me five hundred dollars."

The price was a bit steep, but Don was over a barrel, so he agreed, hoping the guy would remember the conversation once he hung up the phone. Lorne was going into Billings the next day and would settle up the bill. In the meantime, he lent his truck so Don and Irene could go into Wolf Point to get a motel room.

The next morning, Don was pleasantly surprised to find a box waiting for him in the airport terminal: the cylinder had been delivered as promised. Don went to work and had the installation nearly complete by the time Lorne returned later that day with the news that the bill was three hundred and fifty dollars. It turned out that Lorne had torn a strip off the wrecker for trying to gouge his 'friend,' and the price was quickly reduced. The repairs were finished up that night, and the next day Don and Irene left for Edmonton, thankful for the kindness of strangers. "They took us under their wing, loaned us their truck, we used anything in the hangar that we needed, no questions asked. They were very nice people."

The flight to Edmonton was made safely, and Don had accomplished his goal of one last trip back to his hometown: the place where it all began so many years before, where a young man they called Smokey fell in love forever with the dream of flying, and a girl named Irene.

EPILOGUE

Don maintained an avid interest in aviation during his retirement—buying, flying, and selling a number of planes, as well as rebuilding a Stinson 108-3, C-GCRL, with his son Ken, and helping his aviation mechanic grandson Stuart McAulay rebuild Jack Sullivan's Piper Colt G-CLG. Of course he took advantage of any offers to co-pilot with his son, Ken, in the Cessna 195 CF-LEQ, with Jack in the Colt, or with his good friend Burke Fisher in Burke's beautiful PA-12 Super Cruiser, C-FVOD.

Sadly, partway through the writing of this book, Jack fell ill to cancer and passed away on August 25, 2002. Don, Irene, and I continued on with the project, and completed a draft in late 2002.

Smokey Patry died peacefully on April 2, 2004 in Guelph, Ontario. As was his lifelong habit, he had his medal of Saint Christopher at the ready for one last flight.

ALPHABETICAL NAME INDEX

H.J. SMITH was born in Markdale, ON, and currently lives in Guelph. At the age of five he tied a barrel to the basement joists and swung in it pretending to fly. At six he tied an apple box to a rope and pulley and hoisted himself up underneath a maple tree limb, swinging to and fro and "flying" for hours. Smith's first real flight was at age fifteen when he spent all the money he had ($10) for a ten-minute hop in a helicopter over the International Ploughing Match in Bruce County, ON. Years later he earned his private pilot's licence flying with instructors Frank Montgomery (Mosquito fighter pilot, WWII) and Marion Orr (Canadian Aviation Hall of Fame, Order of Canada) from the Peterborough Flying Club. Smith is addicted to airplanes and fly-fishing, habits he supports by working as an agrologist with the Ontario Department of Agriculture in the area of farm environmental education.